W9-AHS-266

Let the Weak Be Strong

Let the Weak Be Strong

A Woman's Struggle for Justice

CHO WHA SOON

Edited by Lee Sun Ai and Ahn Sang Nim

MEYER
STONE
BOOKS

© 1988 by Cho Wha Soon

All rights reserved. No part of this book may be reproduced in any manner whatsoever without written permission of the publisher, except brief quotations embodied in critical articles or reviews.

Published in the United States by Meyer-Stone Books,
a division of Meyer, Stone, and Company, Inc.,
2014 South Yost Avenue, Bloomington, IN 47403

Cover design: Carol Evans-Smith

Typesetting output: TEXSource, Houston

Manufactured in the United States of America
92 91 90 89 88   5 4 3 2 1

ISBN 0-940989-37-9

Library of Congress Cataloging in Publication Data

Cho Wha Soon.
    Let the weak be strong.

    1. Cho, Wha Soon.   2. Methodist Church — Korea —
Clergy — Biography.   3. Church work with women — Korea.
4. Women — Korea.   I. Lee, Sun Ai, 1930-
II. Ahn, Sang Nim.   III. Title.
BX8495.C553A3   1988   287'.6'0924 [B]   88-42730
ISBN 0-940989-37-9

Contents

LET THE WEAK BE STRONG

PART ONE: GROWING UP

PART TWO: CALLED TO PASTORAL MINISTRY

PART THREE: INDUSTRIAL MISSION

REFLECTIONS

Foreword

Lee Sun Ai

I MET REV. CHO WHA SOON in Penang, Malaysia, in 1972, at the General Assembly of the Christian Conference of Asia. She was invited to share her way of ministry with Asian church delegates; I was asked to translate for her.

I had heard so much about her extraordinary way of bringing the gospel to the oppressed and exploited women workers in Korea. Now I encountered her in person; her powerful testimony left an indelible impression on my mind.

Whenever I visited Korea I tried to see her to hear about recent developments in her ministry. During one visit, I suggested that her story should be written to be shared with many. She said that God had given her a gift for oral expression but not for writing.

I made an arrangement for the next visit to go to the mountains with Rev. Cho and Noh Ok Shin. The two nights and three days we spent on the beautiful Mt. Sulak on the east coast of Korea were most challenging and meaningful. I asked some questions and Rev. Cho's spontaneous answers were all tape recorded.

Noh Ok Shin started the work of transcription, which was later completed and edited by Kim Young Ja.

I asked Ahn Sang Nim, the general secretary of the Korean Association of Women Theologians, to look after the progress of the whole project, including translation in English. She was assisted by Marion Kim.

When the English manuscript was completed I discussed it with friends in the U.S.A.: Prof. Letty Russell of Yale Divinity School and Pat Patterson of the Board of Global Ministries of the United Methodist Church. We decided that some complementary articles for Western readers would be helpful.

We are grateful to Prof. Lee Hyo Jae for her article on the social background of Rev. Cho's ministry and the group of Korean women who shared their reflections on the story. Many thanks to Letty Russell for her beautiful introduction and to Pat Patterson for her reflection on the story as an American Christian.

May the deeds and words of this unusual daughter of God inspire many.

Introduction:
Crossing Bridges of No Return

Letty M. Russell

It is no accident that the Reverend Cho Wha Soon ends the account of the first fifty years of her life and ministry among the oppressed people of South Korea with the words, "Now I have crossed the bridge of no return" (p. 138).[1] In her lifetime she has crossed so many bridges of no return it is difficult to recount the many breakthroughs in thought and action that she has pioneered as "a modern apostle."[2] Working to raise the consciousness of students, parishioners, workers, and intellectuals, Cho Wha Soon has often come to points in her own life when she saw things more clearly and began to act according to this new insight. Her reference to crossing the bridge was in regard to the discovery of women's oppression and its linkage to other oppressions, but along the way she has discovered the oppression of rural people, refugees, factory workers, and of the Korean people. She has come to see that structural evil requires a collective movement for change, beginning from the grassroots of society. Thus she says,

> If we really think seriously about the movement and want
> to change ourselves for it, we must go through the pain
> of breaking. The task for the movement of the 1980s is
> for all its sectors to expand and take root from the bot-
> tom, gathering the grassroots people's power. The student
> movement, the Christian movement, whatever the move-
> ment, it must create its share. In fact all the movement
> forces seem to share this same idea. (p. 127)

The "pain of breaking" is what marks Cho Wha Soon's apostleship. Following the footsteps of Christ, she has continued to break free from her social and religious views in order to cross the bridge to the despised women workers in Korean factories. For she found that she could not truly be among her people as a servant unless she repented of her own intellectual privilege and middle-class church traditions and learned to share the wisdom of those at the bottom. In crossing this bridge, Cho Wha Soon has begun to overcome one of the basic contradictions of Korean minjung theology.

This form of liberation theology, which was developed during the 1970s and 1980s in South Korea, begins with the subject of the theology: the *minjung.* In the Gospel of Mark we read about the *ochlos,* the sinners, tax collectors, sick, those opposed to the powers in Jerusalem, the despised people of Galilee, prostitutes, etc., whom Jesus called as disciples. In the same way the *minjung* are those who are " ... politically oppressed, economically exploited, socially marginalized and culturally despised and ignored."[3] They include a variety of overlapping categories of those who have shared in the deep, unresolved suffering, or *han,* of the Korean people. As intellectuals, minjung theologians and pastors are not part of the oppressed underclass of society and usually not part of the women who are "the minjung of the minjung," living at the very bottom. Yet some join the minjung recognizing their mutual oppression as Korean people, and also sharing the imprisonment and suffering that comes out of political struggles for justice, peace, and democracy. Nevertheless, Cho Wha Soon represents a pioneering breakthrough to those at the bottom of society. She has crossed the bridge to women workers and helped open the way to their own self-determination.

A Mother Apostle

Recently one of Cho Wha Soon's disciples presented a talk in my class on her life and its meaning. The talk, presented by Henna Han at Yale Divinity School, was powerfully interpreted by original Korean dances performed by Young Lee, but its most powerful aspect was Henna's own testimony to the way that Cho Wha Soon had become a "God-mother to women laborers in Korea," and a role model for her and for every " ... minister in Third World countries, female and male alike."[4] Cho Wha Soon's motherly love and devotion inspired Henna to speak of

her as a "Motherly Apostle" rather than as a "modern apostle."
As Ahn Sang Nim puts it,

> As we read the story of this remarkable woman what is
> it we can learn about our own mission and ministry? Of
> course, we will each hear and learn different things, de-
> pending on our own context and the particular way the
> message touches our lives. But it seems to me that there
> are some very important insights that might guide us as we
> look for clues to how God has been at work in the life of
> this motherly apostle. The insights I would like to under-
> line here have to do with how we learn to cross bridges and
> open up new insights and actions in our lives, even when
> these may cause us pain and suffering along the way.

A Matter of Feet. Crossing bridges has a lot to do with where
we walk and how we use our feet. Henna Han suggests that
"...doing theology is more a matter of foot than of heart and
brain." But I would think that the exciting thing about Rev.
Cho's ministry is that she made it a matter of heart, brain, *and*
feet! Most often we think that our faith is mainly a matter of
a faithful heart and a strong belief, but Cho Wha Soon learned
from the workers that ultimately what makes a difference is not
just caring or even caring and knowledge of the Christian faith,
but most importantly acting together with the women, putting
your feet and your whole self in their shoes so that you can walk
and work together against injustice and dehumanization.

Cho Wha Soon herself has said, "The most important thing
for a human being is where one should stand to live."[5] In decid-
ing again and again to make her stand with those who are weaker
and alienated, she constantly lives out her theology with her feet.
In her commitment to act, Rev. Cho shares in the usual method
of minjung theology as summarized by Moon Tong Hwan:

1. Experience of the minjung analyzed in terms of socio-
   cultural and socio-economic history;

2. Praxis of action/reflection by standing with the minjung
   and sharing in their struggles;

3. Comparing the experience of the minjung with those in other parts of the world and other previous histories, especially that of the Bible;

4. Story telling as a means of communication of truth that is not abstract and is immediately understandable to the vast majority of the minjung who have little academic education.[6]

The beginning point and the focus of Cho Wha Soon's apostleship is the action/reflection that is possible because of standing with the minjung and sharing in their struggles. We too can make use of this method in our own theology, using similar inductive methods worked out by liberation and feminist theologians in our own nation, but we will also find that the theology itself becomes only words if it does not begin to act on behalf of and together with those who are crying out for justice and human dignity.

Mission at the Center of Life. In acting out her commitment to the oppressed, Cho Wha Soon cast her lot with the Korean women workers in textiles and electronics who had no time off to go to church and could not practice their faith in a middle-class way. Her old view of mission as a form of proselytism in which you tried to convert people into respectable Christians who attended church regularly is graphically presented in the story of the woman worker's agony when told that she would not be saved because she couldn't leave work to attend Sunday service. In discussing this and many other issues with the women, Rev. Cho gradually crossed the bridge to a new understanding of Christian mission and Christian life. Thus she says:

> Isn't the real Christian mission, then, to recover the image of these workers as they were originally created? Mission that begins and ends with the observance of Sunday worship is not real mission. The important thing is to live according to Jesus' teaching, wherever one is, struggling to restore one's rights that were taken by others, to recover one's dignity, and to defend these God-given rights — this is really the true Christian and God-fearing life. (p. 103)

The more that Rev. Cho moved to the center of the lives of the workers, the more she saw how the way one lives out Christ is dependent on the context and situation. The language used, the customs, the life-and-death issues of a particular place are where God calls us to be a worker. This is truly incarnational ministry, a ministry with one's body, which Paul describes as true worship in Romans 21:1. In the same way, we will find that God is present with us in our daily work when we begin to take seriously our own context and surrounding as the beginning of our actions of service and our daily worship. For God's mission to mend the creation and heal the suffering of the world begins right in the center of public as well as private life. Cho Wha Soon cautions us that "staying around the fringes" and refusing to join in the struggle as the "center of life" will result in empty theory and pious talk (p. 107).

Everyone Has to Cross Bridges. In order to grow and change and carry out Christ's ministry where it is needed most, we need to be willing to cross many bridges. Our faith is both challenged and deepened as we learn to act faithfully in changing contexts.[7] Rev. Cho's apostolate was concerned, not only with crossing her own bridges, but also with enabling others to cross their bridges. Taking as her mission the recovery of the image of God and full humanity in the women with whom she worked, Cho Wha Soon began her ministry with conscientization for individual change and maturity, but she soon discovered that individuals who change still become victims of the cruel Korean system of employment and patriarchal oppression. Seeing that the social, political, and economic systems were all linked, she began to conscienticize workers to recognize the social structures that cause the oppression and to work together as a movement for change.

The method she used was one that helped give birth to the women's labor movement and to expand the participation of women in their movement against the powers and principalities of government and multinational corporations. Women's participation in the labor unions grew from 24.4 percent in 1970 to 36.7 percent in 1980, and women staff engaged in unions increased from 22 in 1972 to 425 in 1980. Rev. Cho tells us that the method she used to help spark this movement was one of conscientization: learning to understand the social, economic, and political sources of injustice and taking steps together with others to change them.

The first step to workers' awareness was that of their wanting to become more educated and to *emulate* the intellectuals or students who joined with them. The laborers have a deep feeling of inferiority but gradually become aware of the possibility for change. The second step occurred as the laborers began to struggle for their rights and *to reject* the leadership of the intellectuals as they came to see the economic and social gap between themselves and those they had looked up to as leaders. Finally they reached *maturity* with a sense of their own worth and a recognition of the importance of cooperation with the intellectuals and all groups trying to bring about justice and democracy in Korea and elsewhere.

This continuing process of conscientization for awareness and action moves persons and groups across bridges and through barriers. It is a process that occurs in various forms and ways in our own lives as we grow and change and seek out our own image and calling as children of God. Some of the work we need to do in reference to Cho Wha Soon's story is described by Patricia Patterson in this book. Our own personal response will need to include a new understanding of U.S. foreign policy of neocolonialism in Asia, the ways we contribute to the destruction of women's lives in Korea, and new actions by our churches to oppose this destruction. If any of this sounds too difficult, we have only to turn to the story of Kim Yong Ja's strike to see the power of conscientization as a way of becoming fully human participants in God's mending work.

Standing in Community. In the last chapter of her story Cho Wha Soon describes how she has crossed bridges again and has become a pastor of the Dalwol Church so that she can continue her work of grassroots organizing. Other younger women have come to take up her work among the laborers, and she is no longer allowed by the government to work directly with them or in the factories, so she has moved to a new area of apostolate in a rural area. In seeking to overcome the hostility and suspicion of her new parishioners, Rev. Cho washed their feet with love and care on Passion Sunday and began to find ways to become a Mother Apostle in their midst.

As I washed each one's feet I prayed fervently for that person, mentioning all the life situations he or she was in. As I prayed I wept for love, and all the congregation cried as they prayed. I think it was the initial and decisive event of overcoming their prejudice against me. (p. 141)

This was not a new aspect of her ministry, for Rev. Cho had been caring for feet and for all the needs of persons since her days as a nurse's aid with wounded soldiers at the age of sixteen. Her calling to ministry has led her into the center of community with those whom she serves. And one of the secrets of her deep spirituality is that she finds the comfort of God's love in the midst of those communities of struggle. Cho Wha Soon is never cut off from Christian community, because wherever she goes she creates community through her own willingness to sacrifice and to love. Even in times of imprisonment, in her deep loneliness, pain, and fear, she nevertheless finds courage in her commitment to Christ and to her people to make a stand with those at the bottom of society. Like many other modern and ancient women of courage she discovered that even death would not separate her from God and she stood with the community of faith prepared to die for the truth.

Anyone who makes an unpopular stand for truth and justice knows the pain of loneliness and rejection when the powerful and not-so-powerful alike reject us for our stand. Yet crossing this bridge of no return has its own benefits. On the other side we find new friends and community among those who have taken the side of marginal and despised people. God does not provide us with a guarantee against suffering, but God does promise to be with us among the least of Jesus' brothers and sisters (Matt. 25:40).

The continuing necessity for the practice of liberation spirituality is clear from Cho Wha Soon's own story about trying again and again to have solidarity with grassroots people, and finding herself excluded because of status, education, and fame. But the greatest exclusion was her own sense of pride, and then guilt in that pride, that she describes in the story of her return to the factory after release from prison (p. 123). In talking with Cho Wha Soon both in Inchon and here in New Haven I find that she continues to struggle with the sense of guilt because she has not done enough for those who suffer even more than she. She carries with her a mother's sense of guilt for her suffering children. Ultimately she, and we, have to recognize that the communities of struggle do not look for guilt, but rather for whatever actions we can do in solidarity with them. Standing in community, we are sustained by God's grace and find ourselves surprised by the gracious forgiveness that comes to us from those whom we thought had the least to give. Surely this is a sign that God's spirit is continuing to work in our lives as we stand in community with those who seek to build a new house of freedom.[8]

Christ Among the Minjung

Repeatedly Rev. Cho calls us to learn from Christ and work for the full human image and dignity of every person. Already as a young Christian woman she reflected on questions about the meaning of human life, the causes of Japanese colonization, and poverty among the Korean people, and began planning for ways to *let the weak be strong:*

> I decided to find work that did not necessarily require special talent, but that with earnest endeavor could have results: to live with a loving heart, enduring hardship, sacrificing myself, serving others, and living a meaningful life for my neighbor. (p. 14)

This form of motherly apostolate has borne fruit by conveying the love of God in Christ to many suffering people. Cho Wha Soon's story speaks for itself. Fortunately there were those who knew that many people could benefit from hearing about Cho Wha Soon's life and ministry among the minjung. Lee Sun Ai, one of the editors of this volume, brought the idea to reality by spending countless hours taping Rev. Cho's story and then getting it transcribed, translated, and edited for publication. In sharing the story, the sisters who worked on the project have made a bridge so that Cho Wha Soon could come into our lives and make her witness.

This brief introduction is my way of joining in this witness by sharing a few reflections on what I am learning about minjung theology as it is lived out by Rev. Cho. As a white, North American feminist I know that my perspective and context are quite different from that of a woman like Cho Wha Soon, yet I also know that the only way to have that perspective shifted and opened to new horizons is to open myself to the suffering and pain of my sisters in the Third World. In this need for global solidarity in suffering and the call to bring release for the captives, I discover anew the witness of Jesus Christ and the spiritual empowerment of his ministry (Luke 4:18–21).

In the Reflections section at the end of the book, other sisters have gathered to join in our global conversation. Lee's essay on the social background provides us with essential data on the context of Rev. Cho's ministry and helps us to see that her story is but a small slice of dramatic developments in the history of the Korean people in their struggle for human rights, democracy, and reunification of their nation. Other materials, like the book from Friendship Press, *Fire Beneath the Frost,* also help us to understand the larger picture of the Korean story. In turn, the theological reflection edited by Lee Sun Ai draws us into a conversation with some of our sisters in South Korea as they seek to live out the example and meaning of the story in their own ministries. The global conversation takes on even more specificity for those of us living in the United States as Patricia Patterson shares "The Challenge of Cho Wha Soon: A U.S. Perspective." As the Northeast Asia Secretary for the United Methodist Board of Global Ministries, Patricia has known Rev. Cho and supported her work for many years. She is well qualified to speak of our connections with the Korean people through "bonds of oppression and hopeful struggle for justice and peace."

The story is unfinished, and so is our task, but we hope that enough has been shared to provide a bridge of no return where people from many nations will find themselves working together for the sake of the liberation of the Korean people. Cho Wha Soon's dynamic story of selfless love and critical awareness and struggle against hopeless odds certainly calls us to actions of barrier-breaking love. If theology is in any sense a matter of feet as well as heart and mind (and I think it is), then we will know that we have begun to share the theology and witness of this "Mother Apostle" when our feet begin to move and the story continues in our own actions for peace and justice in Korea, the U.S., and around the world.

NOTES

1. Numbers in parentheses refer to page numbers in this volume.

2. See Peggy Billings et al., "Cho Wha Soon: A Modern Apostle," in *Fire Beneath the Frost: The Struggles of the Korean People and the Church* (New York: Friendship Press, 1984), p. 58.

3. "People of Han," in ibid., p. 9; see also *Minjung Theology: People as the Subjects of History,* ed. Commission on Theological Concerns of the CCA (Maryknoll, N.Y.: Orbis Books, 1983), pp. 35, 142–143.

4. Henna Yeogumhyun Han, "Rev. Cho Wha Soon: A Mother Apostle," paper presented for "Feminist Theology in Third World Perspective," Yale Divinity School, April 2, 1987, p. 1.

5. Quoted by Henna Han, in ibid., p. 14.

6. "Korean Minjung Theology: An Introduction," in *Korean-American Relations at Crossroads,* ed. Wonmo Dong (Princeton: Association of Korean Christian Scholars in North America, 1982), pp. 14–16.

7. See Letty M. Russell, ed., *Changing Contexts of Our Faith* (Philadelphia: Fortress Press, 1985).

8. See Letty M. Russell, *Household of Freedom: Authority in Feminist Theology.* (Philadelphia: Westminster Press, 1986).

Letty Russell *is professor of theology at Yale Divinity School and is ordained in the Presbyterian Church U.S.A.*

LET THE WEAK BE STRONG

PART ONE: GROWING UP

1

Childhood

I WAS BORN IN 1934, when Korea was a colony under Japan and our people were experiencing ever more severe hardships due to the imperialist rule. Though my family's native home for several generations was Yesan in Chungchong Province, my father had moved to Inchon, through Taejon, after the 1919 March First Independence Movement. Because of his participation in the independence movement, my father had a hard time. He was arrested by the Japanese police, but was helped to escape by his cousin — a local government official. He moved to Taejon, but finding the living situation difficult, he moved on to Inchon.

My father lived a very humble and simple life. In spite of the losses he had suffered by leaving his hometown, he worked so diligently that eventually he had twelve horses. Twelve horses can be compared to twelve cars now. Transportation was his business. My father loved his horses very much, and put all his energy into caring for them. He mashed beans to make their food and fed them just as considerately as he fed his own children. Even now I remember that scene so clearly. He was a faithful Christian and a student of Chinese literature. My mother, like other rural women, had no education. She was a sincere Christian, along with my father.

My family was very happy and loved each other dearly. Our living standard was rather high. We had an organ, very rare at that time, and we used to sing together to its accompaniment. Father tried to educate his children according to the Bible. Ephesians chapter 6 was the part he most liked to read. According to its admonition, "Fathers, do not provoke your children to anger," he never scolded us or beat us (Eph. 6:4), and we obeyed our parents (Eph. 6:1). Our family life was very free and democratic. My father was like "Buddha's middle"; he had a good personality and a wholesome character, so everyone liked him. I was always very proud of my father.

When I was seven years old, I went to kindergarten (not common at that time). When I was eight, I entered Youngwha Elementary School, a private school. I was quite talented in art and I always wore pretty clothes. All the studies were interesting for me, and I was very bright and active. I grew up surrounded by the love of my parents, brothers and sisters, friends and teachers.

Much later, when I was working in industrial mission, I realized that my life in my childhood was at a much higher economic level than that of the ordinary people of that time — most of whom suffered under poverty and its tragic consequences.

$$\Psi$$

Even though the atmosphere of my home was very free and democratic, it does not seem to have had any particular influence on my thinking. But from middle school, I began to be aware of a national consciousness. I think this was the influence of the church I was attending at the time — Naeri Methodist Church. The teacher who led our youth group spoke to us about our nation and awakened our consciousness as Korean people. That teacher later became a minister. I began to think deeply about the many issues he raised. Of these, three were serious issues I had to struggle with. First, why does the human being have to live? Second, why were my people colonized by the Japanese people? Third, why were my people so poor? My mind was seriously occupied with these issues. I understand now that these are common concerns for many young people. But they were very difficult problems for me. I used to cry because I could not solve them. My friends teased me, calling me "dung philosopher." Really, I pondered deeply over the smallest matters around me, trying to understand them and their relationship to those three urgent issues.

One day on the way to church, I saw a long line of people

waiting in front of the theater to see a movie, although it was the middle of the day. While looking at them, I suddenly felt pity on them. How come they had so little to do? How could they spend precious time in such a way? Would they ever have concern for the Korean people? I felt such an ache in my mind that I could not help hiding myself in a corner and crying for a long time.

Meanwhile, I was also thinking seriously about what kind of person I should be in the future. When I was a child I dreamed of being a musician, actress, or dancer. Probably this was the influence of people around me who thought I had artistic talent. Then there came another consideration. I was not sure of my talent; I doubted that those dreams could come true. It was only because my home was rich that I seemed to have better prospects than other children. And those were not proper dreams through which to realize my love for my people. I decided to have another dream. I could not yet grasp what it was, but I made up my mind how to live. I decided to find work that did not necessarily require special talent, but that with earnest endeavor could have results: to live with a loving heart, enduring hardship, sacrificing myself, serving others, and living a meaningful life for my neighbor. I set my mind to live for such work throughout my whole life.

Ψ

Finally I decided upon the concrete goal of my life: to develop rural people's consciousness. I was influenced in this idea by the very popular novel *Evergreen Tree* by Shim Hoon. Chae Youngshin, the book's main character, impressed my heart deeply with her pure and sacrificial commitment to the rural development movement. Not only I , but many other aware young students had the dream of involvement in the rural movement. Nowadays, we can compare this to the many young college students who are concerned about the welfare of laborers, farmers, and slum area people. After making up my mind to do rural work, I began organizing a team to prepare for that work.

When I was in my third year of middle school, we formed a team of eight. I suggested the idea first, and those who agreed with it joined the team. We met once a month to study about rural conscientization and to make a plan of action. One idea we had was to select a certain area and have each member act out his or her own role as we imagined it would be. According to this plan we agreed to choose the subject we would study in college. I thought about being a medical doctor, and dreamed of serving a rural area that lacked doctors. We also saved our membership fees every month for the team's action fund. Because we were just middle school students, this was a heavy burden, but we were eager to meet and discuss our plans, spending our youth like burning fire.

However, our group broke up without bearing fruit. A boy and a girl member fell in love with each other, and our team was weakened. The other members, critical of our team's purity, decided to disband. I was very sorry about the breaking up of the team. But even now I have close connections with those friends. One of them went to the rural area and became a farmer with her husband. They sold all of their property and began a night school. They are carrying out social action in the rural community.

2

The Korean War

IN 1950, WHEN I WAS SIXTEEN, the Korean War broke out. When those who have experienced the war begin to recount their miseries and hardships, there are too many to count. But as for myself, in the beginning I did not know much hardship. Our family did not leave with the refugees. Among my family I was the only one to go to Pusan, and when I left home my mood was that of traveller rather than refugee.

Around January 4, 1951, when the Red Chinese army entered the war and the people were again retreating to the south, a thirty-member choir was organized in Naeri Church. The choir members were all my age — fourth year in the six-year middle school system. We soon got instructions from the city that our choir was to serve the nation, that we were to go to Pusan and sing for the soldiers. We had to follow what our nation ordered since it was wartime. As we boarded the big ship, LST, we felt excited and curious, and not at all like war refugees. But when we got to Pusan, the situation was different. The officer in Pusan city told us they had received no word from Inchon city about our coming. The thirty of us suddenly became a group of lost children. We could not go back to Inchon and there was no place we could stay in Pusan. We had no money and knew nobody. Besides, in wartime, who would want to have us? We barely managed to rent an old storeroom, where we all lived together without any choice. Our choir director, Choi Young Sup, ran here and there trying to find jobs for us. Finally, as a result of these efforts our seventeen girl members were employed as nurses in an army hospital. The boys also got jobs, working for the U.S. army.

I became a nurse together with my friends. Because it was wartime, there was a shortage of working hands, so even without any training as nurses we were welcomed. It was called "army hospital," but was actually a school building. All the schools and church buildings had been turned into hospitals to accommodate the large numbers of wounded soldiers, and accordingly we wore army uniforms for our work.

Through my life as a nurse at that time, I became aware of God's calling for me. It was a very valuable period of my life. We were separated into three different rooms for our work: intensive care, regular patients' ward, and "light" patients' ward. My sixteen friends were sent to care for patients in the regular and light wards, while I was the only one sent to intensive care. There I experienced a sensation of life and death mingled together. Some patients had already stopped breathing, some were still alive but just like dead bodies, and others looked on in despair as they themselves waited to die. When I opened the door I could hardly breathe for the smell of decaying bodies. The air was filled with groans of pain and suffering. Foamy spit ran from mouths; there were screams, blood, and sweat, the laughter of mental breakdown.... How can I tell of it all? There was one doctor, one soldier nurse-hygienist, and one nurse's aide in the room. But they were way behind in meeting the patients' needs and treating them properly.

I worked the whole day long, running and serving all the needs in the room. Mostly I helped the patients; dressing their wounds, washing them, feeding those who could not move. It was very difficult and tiring work. By supper time I was utterly exhausted. When I reached my room, I felt irritated because the others' work was sufficiently easy that they still had energy to talk about the things that had happened during the day. They were enjoying themselves, laughing and playing. I complained to God for not being fair to me. I was not any more sinful than others, so why should I have to endure this hardship?

The more I thought about it, the angrier I grew, till I felt I would go crazy. One of my friends understood, and wisely advised me, "No, you should not blame God like that. Instead, you ought to thank God. Who else could endure such hard work, among the seventeen of us? Could Kyung Sook do it? Mi Ja? Mi Kyung? Eun Jung?...Who else?" She went through the names of all sixteen. Finally I realized there was no one among us who could do such drudgery without complaining. "See? You are the only one who could to it. God has especially commissioned the work to you; it seems that you are getting a special favor from God!" That really struck me, and I perceived with new understanding: "That's right! God appointed me specially for this work because I can do it!"

From then on I worked with thankfulness and joy. It was no longer hard. That work proved that God loved me and made me practice the love God had showed to me. I now waited eagerly for the starting bugle at 8:00 a.m. I had used to feel that its sound was dragging me to hell. But now it was a welcome call for me to go to my dear friends. Breakfast, which used to taste like sand, was now honey, because this rice would give me the strength to serve the patients. "Rice is rice, barley rice; Soup is soup, soybean soup. Hurry, hurry up and eat." I sang the tune we used to sing when we were little. My life was full of joy and grace.

Then my relationship with the patients changed wonderfully. They began to call me "Nurse-nim" ("respected" nurse). There was nobody else called "Nurse-nim" among the seventeen of us. Since we were not registered nurses, and were very young besides, they just called, "Hey, come here!" and treated us roughly, as if we were their servants. So their way of calling me had become quite different. Probably they felt love through my hands. I did everything to make them happy. For the bored patients I sang songs, and for those with worries I listened to all their stories. Meanwhile, I encouraged them to have hope in the future by reminding them of their memories of hometown, family, and beautiful things that had happened in the past.

The patients forgot that I was younger than they. They liked me as a mother and sister. One day I looked at the patients lying there with bare feet. It was a cold winter, and the heating was not enough to keep them warm. Looking at their bare feet made me sad. I wanted to make socks for them. I went to the storage room and found some old blood-stained blankets. I took one and went down to the frozen creek with it at night. I broke the ice and washed the blanket in the icy water, blowing on my hands with my warm breath. In the daytime I watched carefully over the patients' food. Then when I returned to my room at night I started sewing socks, continuing until the needle made my finger sore. I could sew about ten pairs a night. I took them in the morning and put them on the patients' feet, one by one. It is impossible to describe how happy they were when I put the socks on their feet. And what wonderful joy I felt, seeing their happiness!

When Inchon was reclaimed, our four months of Pusan life, including nursing, came to an end. We had to go back to Inchon. When we left I received a small sweet-rice cake as a gift, made especially for me by the patients. I cried aloud, and everybody else cried along with me. We felt the sadness of separation.

This was the most worthwhile period of my life, a time of precious spiritual experience. I realized God's love through being chosen for this difficult and trying work, and I was born again. No matter how miserable and difficult one's living situation is, if one is awakened to the real meaning of life, it becomes a beautiful experience.

3

Teacher

WHEN I GOT BACK TO INCHON I found that our economic situation had changed. The education system had also been changed, to three-year middle school and three-year high school. I had to enroll in the second year of high school, but I was not sure my family could support me through graduation. Ultimately, my parents sold our piano for my tuition. I barely finished high school, but I had to give up on college. Again I was faced with anxiety over how to spend my life. I decided to be a teacher in the rural area, according to my continuing dream of rural work. When I met two of my old friends who shared this dream and told them my plan, they absolutely agreed and we decided to work together. Not having graduated from a teacher-training course, we first had to pass the teacher-qualifying examination. We studied hard and all three of us passed the exam.

We were appointed to the Namsa Primary School in Namsamyon, Yonginkun, Kyonggi Province. The people in the area were mostly farmers. Together with another teacher of the school we rented a room in the village and began our communal life. We were lively and dedicated to doing our best in everything. I was responsible for the first-year class and found that my previous experience in Sunday school teaching at Naeri Church was a great help. The school superintendent was an elder of a church some distance away. He favored us because we were Christians and supported us in all our activity.

There was no church in the village, so we asked the superintendent's permission to use one classroom as a church. Without a pastor it could not be a formal church, but our desire was just to have a way to serve the residents and to hold worship services. With the superintendent's glad approval, we started Sunday school. The children liked playing with us very much. During summer we held vacation Bible school, spending our whole vacation with them. In the evening we held a night school, with most subjects being for mothers and youth. We taught Korean writing to the mothers, among whom many were illiterate. In addition, we offered classes in hygiene, child care, and other things needed for daily living. In the young people's classes we taught things related to their studies, and songs. The school had a garden in which we worked every morning, raising vegetables for our food. We worked day and night without rest, but because we were all close friends of the same age with the same hopes, we were filled with joy and passion for our work.

We then began a remedial class for the students who could not keep up with the regular classes. They were mostly fifth- and sixth-year students who had not yet mastered Korean writing. The reason they were behind was that their parents required their help in farm work, and thus they could not find time for study and gradually lost interest in school work. One day when we were teaching this class, one child left to go to the toilet. After a while we heard a scream. We ran out and saw that he had fallen into the open toilet (just a deep hole in the floor). I was shocked, but pulled him out, washed him and his clothes also, and sent him home. While I was doing all this, the other teachers watched me and seemed deeply impressed. They asked, "Are all Christians like you?" Because I was open-minded and cheerful and enjoyed even "drudgery," I was said to be a "comfortable person."

Around that time I was falling in love with a male teacher, which I will mention later.

One day my fellow teachers decided to play a joke on me. After classes I was tired and was about to drop into my chair in the teachers' room. Suddenly one of them pulled the chair out from under me. At that time I was still wearing the traditional Korean dress, and when I fell my skirt flopped open. I hit the floor in a sitting position. I was embarrassed and hurt enough to cry. I didn't know what to do, so just sat on the floor without moving for some moments. I could not figure out how to react. Should I be angry? Actually I was very angry. But as soon as I thought about the teacher who had pulled out the chair, I realized how sorry she must be. They had simply wanted to have fun, but it had turned out differently from what they had imagined. They were all very quiet, surrounding me; I could hear their breathing. It was they who were embarrassed and tense.

I stood up quickly, straightening my clothes. "Hey, what are you doing standing around like this? Did something happen?" "Ahhh..." Breathing deep sighs of relief, they returned to their seats.

The next day, the teacher who had pulled out the chair came to me with a serious-looking face. "I am very sorry about yesterday. But how come a young person like you did not get angry? Shouldn't you have been angry? I really cannot understand." "Well! Actually, I was angry. But if I showed anger, how embarrassed you would be! Thinking of your feeling sorry, I could not get angry." After this event I had another nickname: "One who is not angry, so others won't be sorry." I liked jokes and fun, but on the other hand I was straight like a puritan. Facing injustice, I surprised others with my toughness.

My life as a teacher continued for three years. Then I returned again to Inchon.

4

First Love for Twenty Years

WHEN I WAS TWENTY YEARS OLD and a teacher at Namsa Primary School, it happened that I fell in love with a man for the first time — and perhaps the last. Though he and I were in love for almost twenty years, we could never be married. In fact, we could never even hold hands. "What kind of love is that?" you may say. But I think we shared a really pure and beautiful love.

When we first met, he was a first-year teacher at Namsa school. He was five years older than I and already married. Even though I was always bright and active, I was as strict as a puritan, so even the older teachers did not treat me lightly. I generally avoided private conversations with the bachelor teachers because I was rather popular and I did not want to risk a scandal. But he was married, so I felt freer to talk with him. I simply never thought about marriage; and having no experience of love, I did not know our relationship was love. He always listened to me attentively, even when I said things in fun. Sometimes I noticed him gazing at me like a mindless person while I was teaching the children. When we called on students' homes, two teachers formed one team, and he always arranged to make me his partner so we could go together. On these visits he tried to have me rest while he did most of the work alone. After work he had a glass of wine, then often came and asked me to go for a walk. In the evening we would walk along the tree-lined path and share refreshing, friendly talk. He treated me well but often looked as if he was not quite comfortable.

One day on the way home after visiting students' homes, he asked me, "Cho Sun-saeng (Teacher Cho), you won't stay here forever, will you? If you find better circumstances for the rural movement, you surely will leave. Then you will naturally forget me, won't you? That is ... Even if we are apart, how about your being my adopted sister and I being your brother, to continue the relationship between us?"

"My adopted brother? That's very awkward," I rejoined. I did not recognize this as his expression of love. I did not take it seriously and responded with a joke. Then I remembered that one bachelor teacher had told me, "A married man can fall in love with another woman." But I was so excited and interested in my school work that other things could not matter to me.

Finally, on a study tour, he confessed that he was in love with me. "Coming to know you, I found myself a new person. My marriage life is dead and without love, but you are vivid and make me alive." We did not have any special dates, but just met as we went back and forth in our work. I could feel his care for me. My school life was fruitful and lively, and at that time I thought it was because my goals were pure and I had strong faith. Later, however, I realized it was because deep in my heart I was in love with him and because being with him made me so excited about my work. He also worked diligently. He was not a Christian, but sometimes said that through me he saw God. And he compared me to Mary.

After I came back to Inchon I entered the Methodist Seminary as a student, and could no longer meet him. If I had agreed to our "adopted" relationship as he had proposed, I could have met him with that excuse. But now I had no acceptable reason. Not being able to meet him made me long for him so much it was unbearable. At last I realized that I was deeply in love with him too. Then a letter came from him. He was really fervent but I could see he was trying to control himself. He wrote me love letters three times a day. Each letter was written beautifully, and consisted of five full pages. His letters were so emotional that they very often made me cry. But in any case I had to cut off ties with him since he had a family and I knew our relationship was not right. So I did not reply to his letters. I was alone and sick with a broken heart. Of course he must have suffered just as much.

Three years later I went to the wedding of a friend who had been a teacher with me. There I met him again and we greeted each other with our eyes only, as I was busy helping with the wedding. She was my close friend, and after the wedding I was feeling rather lonely, and I cried. When I got home, what a wonderful surprise it was to find him there. He was greeting my father. He carried on a very lively and kind conversation with

my family, and after a long visit he left. My family liked him
very much and asked about my relationship with him. "Don't
miss the chance to get such a good man for your husband. Get
married quickly!" they told me. I smiled, feeling lonely. I walked
with him that night, and he asked me to meet him again the next
day. But I could not meet him because I was not sure I could
reject him. If he was not a married man I certainly should have
married him. Then I would have had a different life. But I think
that loving such a person was the will of the Lord.

He always watched me with love. That loving gaze was always a mixture of careful consideration, passion, and the agony
of controlling himself. His gaze was with me wherever I went
and whatever I did, following me like a shadow. When I had
been sent to Dokjokdo as the missioner for a pioneer church,
once I became terribly ill. I was living alone and there was no
chance to let my family know how sick I was. I don't know
how he found out, but he sent me a long letter with money for
medicine. Even though I didn't know anything about him he
knew everything about me.

About ten years later, when I first started industrial mission
work, I met him on the street in Inchon accidentally. He asked
me for a date. Since so many years had passed, I felt certain
I could now say good-bye, so I agreed to meet him. The next
day we walked in the park and ate delicious food. I felt myself
losing my certainty. We were together until five minutes before
curfew. When we separated, his image was very lonely, and his
eyes were so full of love it seemed they would melt everything
in the world. I can never forget his eyes, as he walked with
his face turned back to me. My eyes were overflowing with
tears.

After that day I thought about him often, and sometimes I
dreamed of him. In the dream I held his hands, and my body
seemed to float. But I soon woke from the dream. Feeling so
empty, I would close my eyes tightly and pull the sheet up over
my head to have more dreams of him. I could not keep myself
from loving him.

Five or six years passed without my meeting him.

It was in 1972 that I met him again. I was on the way to
the Christian Academy in Suwon for an education program and
went to see my teacher friend who lived near there. She told me

he was in Suwon and said she would arrange for me to meet him. He had continued to work in the education field and by then was in quite a high position. It was lunch hour when we met, and he asked me to go to his home. I had been thinking I would buy lunch for him, but I did not want him to be disappointed, so I followed him. When we got there his wife was out and nobody was at home. With just the two of us, there was a somewhat awkward silence. Then he confessed, "I truly love you. From the first time I met you until now, I haven't forgotten you even for a minute. The agony I have suffered for twenty years is whether I should throw away everything for love: my wife, my children, and all my property. But I find that I don't have the courage to abandon them. It is so painful that I am not able to come to you." I sat, touching the flowers in front of me, as if I had nothing to say, but my heart was pounding. Soon his wife came back. She set the table for lunch. I had seen her several times so we knew each other. After lunch, when I was leaving, he said good-bye, but did not come out — maybe because of his wife. It was she who walked with me and caught a taxi for me. When I was inside the taxi I had the overwhelming feeling that everything was falling down. I finally recognized that our love of twenty years was only like a rose-colored dream. Without meeting him often, I had always kept his beautiful image and lived in longing for it.

But reality is not like that. He became a middle-aged man with everything; nothing could be thrown away. He had a wife, a son and a daughter, a well-furnished house, all settled with all the necessary things. He established his firm status in society. I understood that I had no place to squeeze in there, and I had no intention to do so. I confirmed everything about him and at the same time I confirmed myself. All the emotion was calmed down and cleansed, and the lingering feeling of attachment left. Facing the reality, the beautiful dream came to an end. I was becoming comfortable.

From then on I was able to handle accidental meetings with him without any special feeling. The feeling of love was gone. Besides, there was a gap between his thinking and mine. I knew we had completely different ideas about social issues. By that time I was already in the middle of industrial mission work and was standing against the Park regime. But he was an educator working for the Park regime to produce stereotyped people, as a sincere servant.

One time when I was working most diligently in industrial mission, he came to try to persuade me not to work for Urban Industrial Mission (UIM). Because I was under heavy guard by the KCIA [secret police], I suspected him as an agent. Probably he was not one, and he warned me only out of his friendly concern because my name was being defamed in the papers and on TV and radio. He wanted to advise me not to be involved in UIM so much. I explained my stand sincerely, so by the time he left he had accepted my stand.

After my relationship with him I never had any romantic interest in the other sex. Even if there were a person I might be interested in, it would not last long. I could not get serious about things like that anymore. Because of my own experience with love — as a too-long and difficult journey that ended with separation (but I never regretted it) — I cannot understand young people who start a love affair so quickly and then if anything happens to disturb it, so easily separate and meet other partners. To love somebody and to decide on marriage seems a very difficult matter to me. Is it a usual thing to meet somebody one never knew before and decide to live together for a lifetime? In any event, my relationship with the man I loved throughout twenty years of my youth had a tragic ending. Now, because of my age, as I look back on the agony I went through, I feel it is a precious and beautiful memory. Everything is kept very quietly in my heart. Can a memory always be so beautiful?

PART TWO:
CALLED TO PASTORAL MINISTRY

5

Plain Seminary Life

COMING BACK TO INCHON after three years of teaching life, I was asked by my friend to consider studying theology. She advised me to enter the Methodist Seminary. As I was in a bad situation financially, I hesitated to answer; but in some corner of my mind I wanted to go to seminary and become a pastor.

While I was a teacher in the Yongin area and living with farmers, I often asked myself, "What is the cause of farmers' problems?" We could not grasp the reason from a socio-structural viewpoint as now, but only as a matter of spirituality or lack of morality. Thus I thought in terms of how to recover religious morality. In the rural areas the men gambled in the wintertime. Some lost their whole year's earnings in one gambling session. Their wives wailed but it was no use. Even if someone could help these men financially it would be like pouring water into a bottomless pit. As I watched them I thought that one should live diligently to overcome poverty.

To solve this problem I went to the mountain every day to think and pray. There in prayer I committed myself to live with the farmers. So in that context I was attracted to my friend's advice to enter seminary. However, in spite of her endless urgings, my financial situation prevented me from making up my mind. Just three days before the examination date, I thought, "Anyway, I should at least try to pass the exam." For three days and nights I studied. I was not sure I could pass it. I was not fully prepared, nor did I have the tuition ready. Unexpectedly, after passing the exam, I felt the strong desire to enter seminary. But there was no way I could get the tuition ready, so I had to give up.

Then a very close friend came to visit me and found out my situation. After our talk, she went home without saying anything; but a little later I found a small envelope in the corner of the room. I opened it: it was the tuition money. This friend had lost her father during the Korean War, when he was taken to North Korea by the Communists. As a result, she had become the head of her household, taking care of her younger brothers and sisters and barely making a living. Giving such a sum of money to another was surely not an easy thing for her. Thanks to her help, I did not miss the tuition deadline and was able to enter seminary. She helped me once again with tuition: the last payment before graduation. I have never forgotten her beautiful friendship, and here I express to her my deep appreciation.

After getting into the seminary, I had to earn my tuition for the following semester, so I went to work as a part-time tutor. My home was in Inchon and the seminary was in Seoul. It was a long way, and besides, I had my tutoring work. I finished my seminary classes, then went to tutor, and by the time I got home it was usually 11:00 p.m. or midnight. I had no time to study. When one semester was over, I had to work for the next semester, always under pressure because of the tuition. As the registration date neared, if I was not ready with the payment, sometimes the letters in the book looked like money. English was the most difficult subject for me, and the Methodist Seminary tended to emphasize it. Even now English makes me feel helpless.

My seminary life in general continued without any special incident. Sometimes I fell into skepticism over the reason for my studies. My clearest memory from seminary is my financial hardship; there was nothing else special worth mentioning. I did not even have the chance for graduation preaching. My name was on the alphabetized list to preach — Cho being almost at the end; but then there were some problems in the seminary and our graduation preaching class was postponed several times. Finally I had to replace my planned sermon with a written one. One thing remaining in my memory is that when I was chairing the graduation sermon test, others commented that my voice was unique, that everybody in the back could hear it well, and that it sounded like the rolling of a gem bead. Even now I hear people saying my voice is particularly effective when I speak from a platform.

I entered the seminary in 1956, when I was twenty-three; then I became ill so I rested for two years. In 1961, when I was twenty-nine, I graduated.

6

Dokjokdo

AFTER GRADUATING FROM SEMINARY on December 19, 1961, I was sent to the small island of Dokjokdo, which is located seven hours from Inchon by ship. Sopori Beach, a popular vacation spot, is on Dokjokdo. This small island originally had only a few people, but after the Korean War, notably in January 1951, there was a sudden influx of war refugees and it became very crowded. When I first arrived with my friend, Nam Kyung Hyun, I noticed many small shacks along the shore. Built by and for the refugees, they looked as if they would collapse at any moment. I was astonished to see a great amount of trash, including excrement, littering the whole area. Since there was no toilet system, the road was being used as the toilet, so the village was filled with a bad odor.

I held my nose and looked for the characteristic cross I knew would be atop a church. Far away on the hill I could see a small cross. I ran toward it gladly, but when I got there, I found the church gate nailed shut. Disappointedly I looked in through the broken window, only to find it strewn with excrement. In dismay, I asked a neighbor, "Why is the church in such condition?" "It has been closed for a long time; nobody comes to this church." "Then is there any other church besides this one?" "If you walk along the shore for about five ri (2 kilometers), behind that hill, you will find a church." Kyung Hyun and I started off, asking the way several times. People looked at us like we were monkeys in a zoo. Kyung Hyun was wearing high heels, and the island people had never seen shoes like that.

This church was called Neungdong Church, and it was located in a village of twenty-seven families. Built by the General Assembly, it was a small, pretty church with a tin roof. But when I looked inside, again it was filled with excrement. I felt weak. Again I asked a neighbor the reason. I was told that the twenty-three-year-old *chondosa* (mission worker) had left three

months before, from which time the church was empty of wor-
shippers. It soon came to be used as a public toilet, and then
was closed.

The refugee boat people were superstitious: they were convinced that if anyone believed in Jesus the whole village would
be destroyed. So they even avoided talking to me, saying that
if they got close to a Christian they would have bad luck. Now
this sounds like nonsense, but then it was very serious. I was
astonished by many things. For instance, girls in the village
would squat down anywhere on the street to relieve themselves,
with their faces covered by their skirts and their backsides exposed.

After discussions with the leaders of the denomination, I decided to develop this church. For several days Kyung Hyun
and I cleaned up the building. We removed all the trash and
excrement, washing the floor many, many times and arranged
everything like a church. I decided to offer my whole body to
the task of developing this church. I felt like Chae Youngshin
in *Sang-noksu (Evergreen Tree)*.

After cleaning the church, I was ready for the first Sunday
service. I had written my sermon carefully and was waiting
for the congregation to come. But that first Sunday I had only
one *"dori"* (nickname for a mentally disturbed person), from the
neighboring village of Ssukgae. He sat with a dull expression,
often laughing to himself. I hesitated to preach in front of just
this one person who was not even normal.

I sat down facing him as I pondered what to do, then suddenly I thought, "Did not Jesus suffer on the cross for this very
person? Jesus said he would leave ninety-nine sheep to go and
find the one that was lost. This disturbed man is that very one
to whom I must preach God's word." I then became calm. My
first sermon of my life started this way. For one month that man
was the only one who heard my sermons. Meanwhile, using my
experience as a Sunday school and grade school teacher, I started
a Sunday school. When I met children on the street I invited
them to the church: "You don't have anything to do, do you?
Why don't you come to the church, and I will tell you stories.
We'll have a good time." Since many children had no playmates,
soon there were many children in the Sunday school. Christmas
was coming, so I planned a Christmas program. I taught them

songs, dances, and plays. We brought a pine tree from the hill and decorated it.

On Christmas day, we had ninety-seven people in the church. Most of them had nothing to do in winter and were just killing time at home. So they came to the church to "see the show," since the program had been well-advertised in the village. Most of them were fishermen, so were strong and rather rough. Upon entering the wooden-floored church one should take one's shoes off, but these men kept theirs on. They also smoked, but I could not say, "No smoking in the church." They did as they wished. I was also upset that they had come to look me over. According to gossip, they wanted to see what kind of person this *chondosa* was, looking younger than twenty-nine.

In such an atmosphere I was not sure we could hold the program as we'd planned. I didn't know what to do, but finally decided to change the contents of the sermon. Instead of the Christmas message, I began to preach about fishing people. Jesus loved fishers very much; the first disciple was a fisherman. I earnestly told them the story. Since they did not care about Jesus, they did not seem to be listening at all. However, in the hope that there might be even one person who was listening, I preached diligently. In the middle of my sermon I heard the sound of something hitting the tin roof. Later I found out it was a dead bird, some old shoes, and other such things. I was a little uneasy but tried not to worry about people's reaction and went ahead with the program as planned.

Sometimes young people came to the church, and I told them, "The church is a joyful place for all the people. Please come when you are sad or suffering in agony, or any time; you are welcome here." I am not sure they remembered what I said, but anyway, they came to the church when they had nothing to do and wanted to kill time. I did not force them to believe in Jesus, but tried to be a friend, talking about everyday living and playing games with them. At the Sunday worship service there was only the *"dori,"* as before. Sometimes he came with his sister, and other times with his mother. Even though there were just two or three at most, I continued the worship service every Sunday.

Then Neungdong Church became a sister church of Naeri Church in Inchon. I reported about Neungdong Church to the

Naeri congregation. Since I had grown up in Naeri Church I felt at home there, so I spoke to them about the many hardships and difficult problems just as a married daughter would talk to her mother. I told them about preaching when it was too cold even to open one's mouth, about the lamplight blowing out many times because of the wind, about the difficult event at Christmas time. As I spoke, the tears were running down my face; the people in the congregation were also weeping. Then, without my asking, they took up a special offering for my church.

A large sum of money was gathered, and with it I bought medicine and an organ. Planning to repair the church, I also bought cement. The Naeri Church members brought one boxful of window panes, which had been contributed by Inchon Plate Glass Company. With all the necessary materials, I returned to my church; but there was no one who could do the repairs and no tools to do them with. The people in the village would not let me use their tools because I was a Christian. I had to do the repair work alone. I finally found two young people willing to volunteer their help; one from our church and the other from Bukni Church. So we started on the repairs. I mobilized the children to bring sand from the seashore. I walked in front with a sand-filled washpan on my head and the children followed in line behind me, each carrying a pan with as much sand as they could carry. It was quite a picture we made, walking along the shore. I covered the walls of the church with cement and made it clean-looking.

The next task was the bell tower. As nobody else wanted to go up on the roof, I climbed up myself and put up the tower, with everyone in the village watching. Probably it was an impressive scene for them — a woman up on the roof, working. Later two college students and several high school graduates came to meet me. I shared true dialogue with them and we began to discuss many things together. They also helped with the repairs, which took about a month. At that time I felt as if I were living like a modern Chae Youngshin.

Meanwhile I was thinking about what kind of role this church should play for the village. One thing was very clear: that the church should exist for the development of the community. I started calling on people to become friends with them, calling on homes without distinguishing whether they were those of our members or not, beginning at the top of the village. But nobody was at home during the day. They had all gone out to the fields to work. So — wearing a straw hat and work clothes and holding a *"homi"* (seeding hoe) — I went to visit them in the field nearest the hill. Introducing myself, I began digging, weeding the field with them, and sharing stories. This was the "pastoral weeding call." Trying to encourage the youth to have concern for their village, I raised questions: "Why is this island so poor? What do you think is the reason? Isn't it necessary to find out the reason? What do you think we should do to make this village a better place to live?" I told them, "Let's think hard and make efforts together for this village."

One day, after the word had spread that I was trying to develop the village, the myon (township) official came to see me. He asked me to work for the village. That was in the early 1960s when the May 16 military revolution had taken place and the government was carrying out a booming reconstruction project all over the country. Coincidentally, I was able to have the myon official's support to make my dream come true. I held many public lectures. The contents of my speeches and sermons emphasized daily living problems faced by the village people, rather than the customary "Believe in Jesus and go to heaven." I challenged them to think about what we should do to solve our problems. I also opened a night school, and tried various other projects. From then on, the people looked at me differently. Anyone who met me on the street greeted me; and I became a counselor, sharing dialogue with those who had problems. Even those who had just stared at me without speaking because I was a Christian became my friends.

There was a problem in the village that was a real headache to everyone. This was a gang of twenty-one- and twenty-two-year-old youths who went around and made trouble. They would go into people's homes and harass them for no reason, tease young women, steal rice and sell it for gambling money. One Christmas they took all the *siru ddok* (steamed rice cake) that had been prepared for the church festivities. I was always thinking that I must find a good way to deal with them. One day I was walking along the road when suddenly they were standing in front of me, blocking the way. It was certain they were intending to do something terrible to me.

For a moment I looked at them, then said with a smile, "Hey, do you know how to dance the twist?" "What's the twist?" Their attitude relaxed as they questioned me with curiosity. "Wow, you really don't know? I know the twist well, since I've lived in the city. It's the popular dance of today. If you want to learn, follow me." I walked on ahead of them, but they did not follow.

After some days had passed, I was visited at my room in the church by several of these young men of bad reputation. I joked with them and we played games. They had come to learn the twist. "Okay, the twist is like this. When you drop a cigarette, you rub it into the ground with your foot, right? Use the same form — rub your feet back and forth on the floor and wave your arms, like this." I pretended that I could dance well as I showed them how to do it. They were very excited and had a good time dancing.

From then on they came to my room often, to enjoy dancing or games — even on Wednesday or Sunday when I was busy preparing the worship service. On such a day I could not play with them. "Gentlemen, I am very sorry. Since I have to be ready for the worship service it's difficult for me to play with you now. How about coming back tomorrow?" So saying, I would go into the church. They would follow me in and help me to prepare.

One day they attended the worship service for the first time. By then it was over a year since I had come to Dokjokdo and there were already many members in our church. At the fellowship hour I asked all eight troublemakers to stand up and introduced them to my congregation: "Dear members, these eight men standing here have committed their lives to Jesus today. Let us welcome them as our new members." The sound of clapping hands was like thunder. Our congregation were completely surprised and overjoyed about their change of heart and their coming to the church. The youths themselves were stunned by their reception. They had just come to the worship service without any special motive and suddenly found themselves being treated as sincere Christians. I had deliberately given them a one-sided push.

That day, after the worship service, I organized the youth fellowship with them as the core group. They were stunned again, but seemed excited. I got them to discuss what the fellowship would do for the village, and I participated in the discussion with them. As a result, they decided to open a shop selling daily goods. Without this kind of shop, the people had to go to the next town to buy things they needed. The youth members also went to the mountain and gathered firewood to sell to the "refugees" who needed it.

Even though the war had been over for ten years, those who had migrated to the village at that time were still called refugees. With the money they earned selling wood, the youth group bought daily goods to sell to the people, thereby making their life easier; and with the money from those sales in turn they bought rabbits to raise. I also taught them the nursing skills that I had learned during my wartime experience in the army hospital, to the extent that they could treat minor wounds. Around that time there was an epidemic of boils spreading through the village, but they were successful in eradicating the infection.

The villagers were overjoyed to see these youths — who as idle gangsters had caused so much trouble for them — turned into such fine and reliable young men. Their mothers also became Christians out of their deep appreciation for their sons' transformation, and came to the church. Even now the young people have not forgotten me, and we meet from time to time.

My three-year ministry in Dokjokdo contributed to the education of the illiterate, the overcoming of poverty, and the betterment of people's physical and mental health. Those years were hard, but they were truly worthwhile and exciting years. Through the ministry I was able to realize the dream I had had since I was a child — to be involved in rural development.

7

Healing a Possessed Person

ONE DAY A MAN WHO APPEARED TO BE ABOUT FIFTY came to the church to meet me. I asked him why he had come. "I am living on the other side of this village; I have no right to bother you, but have come to ask you a favor. I have one daughter who is engaged and should soon marry. But she has suddenly gone out of her mind. I don't know the reason. She was all right, then suddenly she lost her senses. If the groom's family hear the rumors, they will break the engagement. It will be a terrible thing to happen to us. I am not a Jesus believer, but I've heard people saying that if one believes in Jesus, mental disease can be cured. I thought that even if that doesn't happen, I won't lose anything by trying; so I came to meet you. Won't you come to my home and pray for us?

I was thinking of myself, "Mentally disturbed? A mental patient should go the mental hospital; why come to the church?" However, I could not really say that to him and instead replied, "Really? Then I will come to your home tomorrow. You did well to come. If you believe in Jesus any disease can be cured. Please do not worry." Saying this in a confident voice, I reassured him and sent him home. But I was really worried. Though there is a story in the Bible of Jesus healing a person possessed by the devil, I had never had any experience of faith healing, nor had I seen it happen. Actually, I did not believe in it. But I had promised to heal a mentally sick person, so I was in a terrible position. I was so worried that I could not sleep at all. All night long I paced up and down restlessly, mumbling prayers. "God, what shall I do? In spite of my inability, I said I would heal her. I am in big trouble. In your name, I am dishonoring you. Please punish this sinner, your servant. Please tell me what to do." My head filled with worry, I finished the morning prayer meeting.

Then, around nine o'clock, a young man whom I did not

know came to see me. I had never seen him before. He introduced himself as a friend of our elder's son, and said he had meant to come and greet me for some time. He remarked, "It must be very hard work for you, serving the church on this island right after graduation from seminary." I said, "It's not so hard." We talked about this and that. Then, while talking about his faith, he mentioned his experiences healing the sick and mentally disturbed! I was completely taken by surprise. "You've really had such experiences?" "Yes, I have."

He said he would return to Inchon the following day. I quickly poured out the story of my problem. "Even though I've graduated from seminary and am working as a *chondosa*, I have never believed in faith healing. Now I have promised to do it. What shall I do? Can you help me?"

He slapped his knee in sudden understanding. "Aha! Now I know why God sent me here. Actually, I had a strange dream last night. I had no reason to come here today, but I kept feeling a desire to come. I happened to have a friend here, so I just came. Maybe I was supposed to meet you. After hearing what you have said, it seems to me that God has sent me to help you. Don't worry about anything. I have to go back to Inchon tomorrow; but let's go to that home tonight. You watch very carefully and do as I do, and everything will work out. I believe I can cure her. First have the worship service, then I will take charge."

That evening a group of fifteen of us visited the home, including several church youth, the senior deaconess, and a deacon. The daughter who was said to be mentally disturbed was light-skinned and bright-looking, twenty years of age. She looked much healthier than I, who was skinny and unattractive. It was hard to believe that such a beautiful girl was mentally ill.

The prayer meeting began. The young lady was sitting beside me, and her twenty-three-year-old brother was across from her. The young man from Inchon sat close to her. We sang a hymn, then I preached, and this was followed by a prayer. We were about to say, "In Jesus' name we pray," when suddenly, with an agonized "Oh!," someone fell backwards. I was so shocked that my whole body felt numb. After everybody had calmed down again, we found that the one who had fallen down was not the girl but her elder brother. He was shouting and twisting his whole body and acting like he was insane. The parents looked shocked and pale. Not only their daughter but also their son had become sick. I remembered that the young man from Inchon had said the night before that the devil sneaks into the weakest one. I had not believed what he said, but it was happening now. The brother was continually shouting and doing strange things. The Inchon man told us to sing hymns and pray aloud continually. We sang "Onward, Christian Soldiers" until we were hoarse. Meanwhile, the young man sat in front of the brother and began to talk to the devil that was in him.

"What kind of devil are you?" The devil answered through the brother. "I am a Tosan devil." "Where are you now?" "I am in the backyard." The young man from Inchon was yelling in a voice of authority and the disturbed man was trembling as he answered. It was very mysterious. The young man asked me to go to the backyard, find what was there, and destroy it. Saying to myself that this was something "to make the devil cry" (that is, it was impossible to believe), nevertheless I went to the backyard. There I found a small, house-like structure. When I opened the door I saw a small box, inside of which were placed pieces of red, yellow, and royal blue fabric. On top of the cloth there was new money, both bills and coins. Set neatly in front of the small house were a bowl of rice and a cup of water. I was told that the family changed the rice and water diligently every morning.

I burned them all. As I came back to the room, the man's symptoms seemed less, but soon he got worse again and behaved like a deranged person. The young man spoke again. "You, devil, where is the other place you are living?" "I am living under the floor." I searched under the floor and discovered white paper stuck on the wood and something wrapped in white cloth. I opened the cloth and saw a paper on which something was written. I took them all out and burned them and came back to the room again.

Now the young man asked the devil, "Who is the most fearsome person with the strongest faith among us?" That moment I was frightened. I was afraid the lips of the possessed man would say, "The *chondosa* is a sinner with no faith." Actually, until then I had not believed in this kind of action and had never thought the illness could be healed in this way. So it was inevitable that I would be called "one with no faith." I remembered the Bible verse telling how the one who first confessed Jesus to be the son of God was possessed by a devil. If that were true, it would be disclosed here that I was a faithless *chondosa*. How shameful! I even felt that it was nasty of the young man to ask such a question. If the possessed man should shout, "What kind of *chondosa* is she who does not have faith?" then I would have sneaked away from the island at daybreak the next day. I would have been too ashamed to face the island people.

My head was filled with complicated thoughts, my heart was pounding, and I scarcely dared to breathe, as I sat with bowed head, supporting the possessed man's shoulders from behind. Then he spoke: "This woman who is holding me from behind is the most fear-inspiring and most faithful!" I was astonished. I, the most fear-inspiring one? Without intending to, I sighed, "Oh, Lord, thank you," and drew a long breath. I have never, before or since, felt such relief as I did then. I repented my faithlessness. But the fact that God had chosen me, a person so lacking, filled me with joy and gratitude. I confessed that I would follow whatever task God set for me to do.

"Who is the next?" the young man from Inchon asked. "You who are questioning me are rather frightening. And you, deacon treasurer, if you want to be a Christian, be a good one! You are Christian soldiers? Ha! A hundred of you, come on! I won't even blink an eye!" The possessed man laughed scornfully. Now I was convinced that I could heal the young man's sickness. God had chosen me in order to use me as a servant; therefore, as long as God was with me there was nothing I could not do. Trusting the biblical promise, "Through prayer, nothing is impossible," I found that my negative attitude was changed to a positive one.

From then on my fears disappeared and I could talk with the possessed man. He sometimes recited poetry, and at other times made such statements as "I brought ruin to this house." Later I heard from his family that they had had a business selling tiny shrimp preserves. On one occasion they had arranged to deliver twelve drums of preserves to Chungchong Province, but by the time the shipment reached there, the preserves had all spoiled. This was the start of the family's decline.

I prayed five days and nights for the young man. It was winter — the coldest winter in thirty years, and I was wearing many layers of clothing because I was not healthy and could not stand the cold. But I was praying so hard as I sat with the young man that all my layers of clothes were soaked with sweat. I prayed to God, "If need be, take my life and heal him instead." There were people who gathered to watch what was going on. I had to show them a miracle. In this island where superstition prevailed, it was the only chance to remove such wrong beliefs. I prayed sincerely with all my heart and strength.

After a few days I had him kneel down and bow his head, but his head would not stay down. I pressed it down hard and told him to say "God," repeating after me. He could not say the word "God," or "Jesus;" it came out as "G-G-G-G-God," "J-J-J-J-Jesus," with the sweat pouring down his body. Worn out from trying to make him say "I will believe in Jesus," I was resting briefly, when he came back to himself for a moment and described what was happening to him. In front of him was seated an old man in white clothes, he said, who was yelling, "Why are you bowing your head to God? Don't turn away from me!" When he tried to bow his head the old man would hold his chin up, and when he tried to say, "God," the old man held his mouth shut. If he called to God constantly, then the old man would appear to be suffering and would leave. Then the young man would return to himself.

He would seem normal, then have another spasm, then seem better again. On the fifth day, at last, the young man wept unrestrainedly and said, "Since this household treats me so badly, there is no way but to get out of here." I replied, "Then you must go to hell." The devil in the man said, "It's not time to go to hell yet." Upon which the young man recovered his normal self completely.

This experience was a very precious one for me. Long afterwards, I sometimes found myself wondering whether this might have been just an accidental happening with no relationship between my prayers and the young man's healing. But I was again convinced that God had been with me then. From that experience I developed the firm faith that — together with God — I could overcome whatever hardship might confront me. That conviction gave me the strength to endure later on, when I was speaking from the pulpit and suffering under government oppression. Even now, I firmly believe that God is with me, and I live on in the strength of that faith.

8

Dalwol Church

THE PIONEERING EFFORT AT DOKJOKDO CHURCH had originally
been planned to last five years, but the General Assembly decided to shorten that, and therefore I was sent to Naeri Church
in Inchon, as an educational assistant. However, Naeri Church
had various problems, so after some time I was sent on to Dalwol Church. This church was located in Kyonggi Province (Kun-
jamyon, Wolgonri), about a one-hour drive from Anyang. Its
residents lived mostly by rice and vegetable farming and salt
farming. The church membership was about twenty.

However, I found that Dalwol Church had a problem: a
conflict between the former *chondosa* (mission worker) and the
congregation. When I got there, I could understand why. The
former *chondosa* had many problems. Although he had been
assigned to another church upon my assignment to Dalwol, he
was insisting on staying there. He was a Korean War refugee
who had studied some Chinese but had no theological training.
He was able to draw church members by his acupuncture skills.
Even disregarding his outward appearance, he was so rough and
uneducated that the church members called him "gangster *chondosa*." Because the congregation disliked him so much they
appealed to the General Assembly to send him away. But he
rejected the order to move and insisted on his right to stay,
based on his contribution to increasing the church membership.
Furthermore, he was unwilling to move to the assigned church
because it was in a worse condition than this one.

Under these circumstances, the General Assembly intentionally sent me, a woman. If the new *chondosa* had been a man, an
even more serious fight might have taken place. I had a conflict
with him every day; it was terrible. He seemed determined that
I should leave, but I could not do that.

Then an incident took place. The *chondosa* called a meeting
to stir up the townspeople who were not our church members,

in an attempt to make me leave. He got up on the platform and criticized me very harshly. After watching the scene for some time, I went up on the platform and explained the facts: "Dear people! The things this *chondosa* said were not really true. I did not come to take away his position. Dalwol Church belongs to the Methodist church so has to follow Methodist law. I came here according to the Methodist law, being sent from the General Assembly as a *chondosa*. I have a duty to serve this church. If I were seeking personal gain, there are other places with better conditions than this. I have heard that my salary will be 2,000 won. I am a seminary graduate. I could earn a salary of 2,000 won even as a housemaid. His accusation that I came here to kick him out for the salary is nonsense. Frankly, I did not want to come here, but I have made a vow to God to be a *chondosa,* so I had to follow this way. Likewise, he does not want to go to another place but he must go. Having made a vow of service to God, he has no choice."

There were some changes in the atmosphere; the people seemed to understand me. The "gangster *chondosa"* had never persuaded people calmly. He dominated them forcibly so that they were sick of him. Upset by the changed atmosphere, the *chondosa* suddenly grabbed me and threw me off the platform. I almost fell and was so shocked that I laughed. One of the village people, looking on at all this asked me, "Is the law really like what you said?" "Yes," I replied, and the villager left. Then another man left. One after another, everybody went out. Only the *chondosa* and I were left. He looked like he was in a daze.

As the village people had turned away from him, a few days later he sneaked away early in the morning. Not only did he escape, but he took all the church property with him. Even the rice I was supposed to eat he took away. I was left with nothing to eat. I could not say to the congregation, "The *chondosa* took my rice." But I did not starve. A strange thing happened every morning. I would hear cautious footsteps just before I went to morning prayer meeting. When I came back I always found a handful of rice in the corner of the wooden floor. With that rice I could survive. At first I did not know who brought it, but soon I found out. A former member of the church had married into a Buddhist family. Having left her Christian home for a Buddhist home, the newly married woman could not resist her in-laws' religion, but as an expression of her faith she brought the rice offering to the church every morning. (Korean churches traditionally have such a rice offering for the pastor's meals, taking out a spoonful of rice for each member of the family, in prayer, before preparing every meal.) Anyway, with God's care, or her help, I could survive. Later this woman became mentally disturbed. She could no longer stand the Buddhist atmosphere at her in-laws. Thus the family inevitably had to look for a church, and I came to have a relationship with them. That was the turning point for the family to become Christian. Her husband was very faithful and is now serving the church as an elder.

The Dalwol Church ministry was a great success. I worked hard, reflecting on my Dokjokdo ministry experience. Everybody liked me very much. The membership increased from twenty to 150 in three years. In March 1966, I was ordained as a pastor of the church. I was there until October of that same year.

9

Beginning the Work

THE NEWS SPREAD that I was doing well at Dalwol Church. One day I received an unexpected visit from an American minister named George Ogle. I wondered why an American had come all the way to this rural area. In a comfortable way that gave me a good impression, he explained, "I am a Methodist missionary from the United States. I am doing God's work with laborers in the Inchon area. They are the oppressed and marginalized in our society. If Jesus were alive now, he would be with them. We call mission work in laborers' society, 'industrial mission.' For industrial mission we need good workers, and we would like very much for you to help us."

Rev. George Ogle had come to Korea to do industrial mission, invited specially by the Revs. Cho Seung Hyuk and Won Chang Duk, to assist the Inchon area mission. Rev. Ogle had not only had experience in urban mission in Chicago, centered in the church, but had also taken a three-month industrial mission training course at McCormick Theological Seminary. When he came to Korea in September 1961, the Inchon industrial mission work had just begun that spring. At the beginning the pastors used the usual evangelical method, having dormitory prayer meetings and worship services during lunch hour. After Rev. Ogle came, however, they began real industrial mission. It would not be an exaggeration to say that industrial mission in the Inchon area started in September 1961 after Rev. Ogle's arrival.

I refused his suggestion at once. I was having a great time

with my ministry. Why should I be bothered with industrial mission, which I did not even know about? Rev. Ogle nevertheless persisted, coming to me several times and trying to persuade me of the importance and necessity of industrial mission.

At about that time I was approached with offers of three new positions: one was that of missionary to Japan, the second was a school chaplain's post, and the third was the industrial mission proposal. In any event I did not want to leave Dalwol Church. At first, the congregation was also against the idea of my leaving. Then later they changed their attitude and told me that whatever I decided it was up to me. "We cannot hold a fine minister like you in this rural church. For your development you should go to a better place where you make a bigger contribution."

I decided to leave Dalwol Church. Because I had not made any preparation for a move, I did not know which position to choose. I rather favored the idea of choosing the most difficult place. Then Rev. Ogle came for the fourth time. He talked a lot about the industrial mission. As I was showing some interest, finally he said, "To be an industrial mission worker there is one necessary course to go through. That is, you — Rev. Cho — must enter the factory to train yourself by working together with the laborers. The course requires at least one year for a man and six months for a woman. This is the stage at which most of those who have decided to be industrial mission workers fail to come through. How about you, Rev. Cho?"

I felt my ears open wide, and my mind became clear. "Why didn't you tell me that before? If others think it hard work then I will do it. I sincerely think I should do the hard work that others do not want to do." Rev. Ogle was surprised and fascinated by my words.

I did not need any second thoughts. I did not want to be a missionary to Japan. With my experience of colonial life under Japanese imperialism, I was sick of the very word "Japan." The school chaplaincy seemed too comfortable and simple a position. But now I had heard that industrial mission was hard work, so wasn't it the right work for me? My parents were against the idea. "You had a hard time finishing your college education and becoming a minister! Why should you choose the labor field?" My father was so angry that he said he would excommunicate me — remove my name from the family register. My mother even passed out, she was so upset over the matter. But finally I dared to step into industrial mission, on October 6, 1966, against all opposition.

ψ

The office of Inchon Industrial Mission in Hwasudong, Inchon, was a straw-roofed house. It was here that I started my new life when I left Dalwol Church. For the first month I stayed in the office reading reports and new theological books to overcome the conservative faith that I had held until then. Bonhoeffer's *Letters from Prison* impressed me very much. Rev. Ogle taught me many new perspectives and methods and urged me to renew my commitment. My field training spot was Dong-Il Textile Company, which was located in Mansokdong, Dongku, Inchon City.

Rev. Ogle was the one who contacted Dong-Il Textile Company to arrange for me to enter the company, but things did not happen smoothly. During the delay, I was able to have one month's orientation period.

This field training was influenced by the French worker-priests, and ministers who want to do industrial mission consider it very important. Such a working-training program is a very good experience, enabling the minister to identify with the laborers, understanding their thoughts and actions and the process of their work, even though this is only a temporary experience.

The Inchon Industrial Mission was unique among industrial mission efforts. Recognizing that industrial mission needed new attitudes and methods, it attempted new approaches apart from the pastoral ministry. The industrial mission workers went into the factory directly, where they attempted experimental action, then made plans for future action based on the results of their experiments; during this process they developed their theology of mission to the laborers. The main efforts in industrial mission at that time were this one sponsored by the Methodist Church, the Youngdeungpo Industrial Mission of the Presbyterian (Jesus) Church of Korea, and the Dong-Il Industrial Mission project of the Presbyterian (Christ) Church of the ROK.

In November 1966, I entered Dong-Il Textile Company, with

Rev. Ogle's introduction. Among the more than 1,400 workers, I was a stranger, having never been in a factory before. First I was led to an office where I was to receive my work orders. The man in the office told me to wait for a moment, but then he did not come back for two hours. Knowing nobody and left alone there for over two hours, I felt "as helpless as a borrowed barley sack." It was my first experience in the factory and I could not bear it. I felt completely ignored and alienated. Having always received recognition before, as lovely daughter, then as teacher and minister, now I was being treated like this! How unbearably insulting!

When I had waited for this long time, finally the man came back and took me to the storage room. There he gave me my work uniform and cap. The cotton uniform was overly large and wrinkled. When I put it on and looked in the mirror, I felt like crying. How terrible I looked, so small and shabby! I ordinarily had a slight inferiority complex, as I am short and not good-looking. But with the right combination of clothes I could look attractive. Now, in the ugly uniform, my ugly shape showed as it was, and I felt timid and miserable. I thought, "This is what it's like to fall from a minister's position into a worker's position!"

My first work assignment was the kitchen. Most of those who were working there were widows in a welfare program. They seemed to be about my age or younger; I was thirty-four. The man who brought me there introduced me unceremoniously, "Here's a new worker — try to get along well with her," and went out. I did not know what I was supposed to do, so hesitated. Then suddenly a woman shouted, "Hey, you! Come here!" I was stunned. I had never seen her before; how could she talk to me like that? All my common sense resisted. "Hey, come here and wash the dishes!" I had never before been ordered around like this, nor treated as a lower being. I felt I could not bear it. I realize now that it was a hidden sense of superiority that made me feel so angry. With mixed feelings, I began washing the dishes. Soon, however, a woman yelled, "Hey! I'm busy here, so why are you stuck there? Come over here and do this first." I hurried over and did as I was told. Then from the other side came orders, swearing and shouting. I did not have one set position so I was "ping-ponged" here and there. It was a miserable experience. I worked like this in the kitchen for three weeks. Then I worked in the factory proper for three weeks in each department.

From the kitchen I went to the *"jungpo"* department. Jungpo is the final process of textile-making, where invisible mending is done. The workers there had a higher educational level than the others, and that is probably the reason they seemed to feel superior and tended to look down on other workers even though we were all workers together. I had to bear teasing and scolding from workers who were as much as ten years younger than I.

Even in that kind of situation I was thinking that I should evangelize this factory. Wasn't the purpose of my coming here for this working-training to lead these workers to God? It wasn't just for the purpose of labor itself. "Young lady, how old are you? Where is your hometown? Are your parents living?" With a friendly smile, I tried to talk to my younger workmates, while keeping my own hands busy. I was interrupted immediately by the sound of a whistle from somewhere. Startled, I looked in that direction to see the supervisor pointing his finger at me and shouting, "You, who are here for the first time! Why do you have so much to talk about?" It was my first time to be insulted in front of so many people. I was so ashamed that I told myself, "I will quit tomorrow! Why do I have to continue this work if I am to be so embarrassed and scolded?" Even though my hands were still working, my mind was struggling with many complex thoughts.

That very same afternoon, another humiliating thing happened. I was working hard, and this time there was not only a warning whistle but someone shaking my shoulder and berating me, "What kind of working attitude is this? If you don't like to work, get out of here!" I was doing my best so did not know what was wrong. Later I found out that I was not holding my body straight as I worked; being unfamiliar with the work I was bent over a little, which was a bad working position.

I was furious. I hated the supervisor enough to kill him. Then I remembered what Rev. Ogle had said. "This working-training is not to evangelize workers but to do the work itself. You, the minister, do not have to evangelize them anew. God is already with them — working now, right there in the midst of them. Your work is to help them see God within themselves. And the working experience is your most important training to

learn their way and order of life. You will find God working
through all the labor process."

Aha! That was it! Not till then did I realize the meaning of
what Rev. Ogle had said. Suddenly I was burning with humiliation as if I had been struck with a hot whip. I was the person
who was preaching "love" every day from the pulpit. Not ordinary love, but Jesus' love. Then what was Jesus Christ's love?
His love led him even to die for the many people of the world
who do not know their own sin. He was God's only son, son
of the Most High, but he came down to the lowest position and
did the very lowest work, and even died for these others. "But
look at me, I who call myself the servant to the Lord and even
became a minister, what am I doing now? I am not the only one
doing this work. All of us in this factory are working together.
Then why should only I feel it unbearable? Isn't it because I
just want to be served?" Hadn't I gotten accustomed to being
served by others as a teacher and minister? Jesus said he did not
come to this world to be served, but to serve. Did I ever have
a mind to serve? I thought, "I must come down like Jesus. I
have to come down to the bottom. I have to give up myself, and
then I may serve others." I became humbler than before, feeling comfortable and broad-minded. With such an open mind,
and living with the workers, I could newly understand all the
problems that before I had viewed negatively. I was filled with
a feeling of indescribable love.

Now I could understand the workers' fighting for no special
reason, swearing and pulling hair and hating each other. When
I had first seen this kind of happening I had felt disgusted and
said to myself, "They're ignorant; it's hopeless." But now I came
close to them and listened to their stories about their lives, so
I could understand their actions. If I were in their situation I
would be the same. Living on a "rat's tail salary" [a salary far
below one's living expenses], they were exhausted in body and
mind.

Out of her salary a typical worker sent money to her home
in the rural area to buy a pig (to raise for income), she put
some into a savings account, and sent some more home for her
brother's school tuition. Most workers sacrificed themselves for
their families. But when a girl worker returned home for a visit
she was as likely as not to find her drunkard father smashing

up the house and beating her mother. Even though she worked so hard to help out at home, it was like pouring money into a bottomless pit. In this situation, it was no wonder that workers often wished they could die. Under such circumstances it was natural for anyone to get irritable; in fact, anyone who acted gentle and refined was probably not normal.

My new understanding turned into compassion, and this compassion developed into love. I sincerely repented my whole life so far. I decided that from now I would live for the workers. Through this experience I realized the meaning of incarnation theology as Rev. Ogle had explained it, and I newly found Jesus Christ. I had a new feeling toward everything, every relationship, and every word. Every experience came to me as fresh and vitalizing. I was reborn. I promised God sincerely, "Even though everybody else leaves them, I will not leave them; I will live a life together with them."

Ψ

After six months of this kind of field training, though it was insufficient, I felt I had a basic feeling for the workers' situation. Their most important problems were related to sex, recreation, and salary. I thought I should start from these kinds of issues when I planned programs for them.

It was nearly December, and I made plans to hold a gathering for the Dong-Il Textile workers. A Christmas party would make them happy, especially those lonely ones who had no place to go at Christmas; and this could lead to future programs together. I suggested this plan to the workers. They agreed it was a good idea, and forty of them said they would come. I made the invitations and sent one to each worker. I chose Naeri Church as the party place, and the church members prepared *ddok* (Korean rice cake) and gifts for the program.

Christmas day arrived. I was very excited, preparing this and that, and waiting for the invited workers. But somehow, the guests did not show up at party time. I was puzzled. After I had waited for two hours, seventeen of them arrived, but no more came after that. The program had been carefully planned for an exciting time together. I asked the workers, "How come the other friends who said they would come are not here?" They answered, "Sister, it's because you chose the church as the party place. How can we come to the church only for the Christmas party? Shouldn't we then attend church continuously? That makes us feel an uncomfortable burden. And why is there no fee? Are we beggars? Come to the church for *ddok* on Christmas? We would rather pay and eat with dignity. Since there's no fee, and since the party is in the church, the others didn't want to come."

I felt like I'd been struck on the head. I was still not letting the workers be the center; I was trying to do things my own way, and I hadn't overcome the church-centered tendency in planning programs for them. And one more problem was that I did not realize I was trying to offer something to them. Actually, subconsciously, I was feeling intrinsically superior, thinking I was in a better position than they. They were more self-identified than I; they had a sound will and were reluctant to receive anyone's favor without paying for it. I realized that my attitude of offering was sound neither for them nor for me. I had to help them stand on their own and do everything by themselves. This experience of the Christmas party provided an important example for me that I remembered from then on, whenever I planned education and action programs, counselling, or other activities.

10

Dong-Il Textile Struggle

THE DONG-IL TEXTILE COMPANY was established during the Japanese colonial era and is now a prominent enterprise in the textile industry. The labor union, formed in 1946, was active until the May 16 (1960) military coup; after that it functioned for the government, not for the laborers. It has 1,300 members, among whom more than two hundred are men and the rest — over 1,000 — are women. Because I began industrial mission work at Dong-Il Textile Company, I have a deep relationship with the union. My relationship with the laborers is like that between parent and children; even after eighteen years, our bond remains just as strong. Their struggle for the democratization of their labor union has continued for eighteen years, and I have been with them. I changed their life and they changed mine. I thank God for this, believing that my meeting with them was God's will.

After my field training I began my industrial mission activity, using three methods in parallel. The first was handing out "calling bulletins" in the factory, the second was visiting the workers' homes, and the third was organizing group activity and labor education. The calling bulletin — used since the beginning of the Inchon urban industrial mission — was one part of factory ministry, which meant regarding the company as a church and serving it accordingly. A mission worker assigned to a particular company would visit the workplace, hold worship services, dialogue with the workers, and hand out the bulletins. The contents of these were based on Christian thought; they avoided an excess of religious color, while presenting interesting, useful stories.

I used the bulletins as a medium for dialogue with the Dong-Il workers. The workers liked Thursdays, when I came to visit them. They called me "Thursday Auntie." ("Auntie" is a familiar name for a person around the age of one's aunt.) But frankly, I did not like to go around distributing the bulletins; this activity made me feel embarrassed. So, on Thursdays, as I was on my way to the company with the bulletins, I prayed — for courage to do my work well. When the workers first received the bulletins, they made fun of them, but later they showed their sincere appreciation. I always went around with a smiling face, and my gentle and open appearance made them like me.

One man worker said he and his wife had been having a quarrel and he did not even want to look at her, so he turned his face away; then he remembered my happy face, which made him smile, and his smile led them to reconcile. Another worker said he took my bulletin home, and every morning at the breakfast table he read it for the children's education. Distribution of the bulletin brought good effects in general. Through the bulletin I became familiar with all the workers in Dong-Il Textile Company. We cannot imagine such a situation now, but at that time, in the late 1960s, it was possible. That was at the beginning of industrial mission and before the labor issue became a general social issue. In fact, it was often the company side that asked the industrial mission for programs for the workers.

Another activity of the mission worker was calling on workers' homes. I did such calling often, sharing dialogue with them. Sometimes I prepared questionnaires for use during conversation, to find out the level of their awareness. I visited mostly in Mansokdong, where I was shocked greatly by the awful poverty. I perceived my comparatively comfortable life up to then as a sin, and I thought that in order to atone for it I should live together with the workers for the rest of my life.

The houses where the workers lived were shacks that looked as if one strong gust of wind would blow them away. They were mostly two-story, ramshackle wooden houses, with six or seven workers renting each room. The rooms were built inside and outside of the house, wherever space was available. Not only was the small space under the roof used as a triangle-shaped room, but the second floor was subdivided again into two layers, making another set of rooms close to the ceiling. There were no toilets inside the houses; rather, straw bags were strewn on the beach for that use, but even they were scarce in number. The village smelled terrible. Because the straw bags were few, there was always a long waiting line every morning.

Housewives in Mansokdong were continually looking for ways to earn money, but there was no work for them to do. However, just offshore, floating in the sea, were a quantity of logs waiting to be processed by the Daesung Lumber Company, which was located there. The women would sit astride the logs and peel off the bark, then sell this as firewood. In this way they supported their living in a small way. Daesung Lumber should have paid them for this work, but they never got a penny. Moreover, there were occasional accidents when women would fall into the sea and drown. The women could sometimes also find oysters at the shore and sell them for income. The typical worker's meal was soy sauce, tiny pickled shrimps, and bean sprout soup with rice. *Kimchi* (the most popular dish in Korea) was on the table only when they had extra money to buy it. The only method of savings available to them was to reduce their food intake. They lived in extreme poverty. But one thing no house was without was a bottle of medicine. This was for stomach trouble, which afflicted most workers due to their working three shifts.

Through this visiting activity I could understand their lives more concretely and feel their pain. I came to believe that my faith would become perfect by my living with them.

At the mission center we organized a group centering around those who had come to the Christmas party. We held group meetings and began an education program with lectures twice a month. The lectures focused on themes chosen by the workers: meeting the opposite sex (this was the subject of most concern), knitting, cooking, handicrafts, flower arranging, home etiquette, etc. However, even though the workers wanted to participate in the program they were working in three shifts, so that all of them could not come at the same time. So we divided them into three groups according to shifts.

As the lecture program brought a good response, we divided it according to subject, with each subject again divided into three groups (because of the shifts). This made thirty groups; and within two months the members numbered more than two hundred.

Through this lecture program the workers were vitalized in their everyday life; the factory atmosphere was brightened, and production increased. A man came from the company to thank me for these positive results, and asked me to help to plan such a program center in the company. Therefore, in 1967–68 I went into the company and organized the program for them, thanks to which I became friends with all the workers of the company. Later, however, when I was opposing the company, I was prohibited entry.

The small-group education program was changing by itself as time passed. When the workers gathered, they talked about their lives and their work. In the process of their conversation, there was often mention of unjust treatment, so the workers came to realize common problems related to their work. While I listened to their talk, I was pondering how to solve their problems. I thought about a labor union, but I did not know much about unions yet. Anyhow, to those who were pouring out their dissatisfactions, I said, "Let's worry and work together to solve these problems."

I raised this issue at the staff meeting, and it was decided to start labor education. This was an exceptional decision for that time, because labor education had always been for the union staff — most or all of whom were men. Not only lay union members but also women workers were outsiders to labor education.

The first task we gave them was to do a survey of the factory. Next we held lectures on "What is a labor union?" and "What is the labor law?" Then they studied the history of labor unions and social-economic history. The workers discovered that they had a labor union in their company; but as it was pro-government, it did not represent them. Furthermore, they found that all the local committee chairpersons were men, who were not concerned about the suffering of the majority who were women workers, but only negotiated with the company for their own benefit. The workers thereby came to the conclusion that in order to represent women's voices, they needed a new labor union formed by the women. Before going on to action, we had emphasized labor education, along with the women's issue. To complete their chosen task, the workers had to overcome their passivity and attitude of resignation.

The workers gained self-confidence. Each group decided to work out a strategy to "turn the union upside down," forming a new union through the process of election of delegates. I led each group in examining the subjects: "What is an election?" "What kind of person should we choose as local chairperson?" and "What is the concrete process of voting?" One group generally had eight to twelve members. Each of these members was told to go out and educate, in turn, one other worker, who would continue the process. In this way, without the company knowing, the hope spread among the workers that "this election will be a democratic one, and we will make a real labor union that speaks for us."

Prior to this, the union elections had been handled completely by the company from start to finish. As the workers went along with whatever the company wanted, the union existed for the company. The company would choose a person they could handle, and with money and promises of promotion would make him vow to be loyal to the company. Then he would be presented as a candidate. Every section had its candidate named in this fashion, so that the election was controlled. The workers voted for the person named by the company, thinking that voting was like that. Just as the delegates were selected, so they in turn voted for a chairperson favored by the company.

Now the industrial mission members were enlightening the other workers about how to have a new union really representing their interests, and this was an exciting project for them. We even carried out a "practice" election of the delegates we wanted to have. Since the group members were already organized by section, it was easy to have such a practice vote. We decided to have each group choose one delegate, through discussion and vote. In all, twenty-four delegates were chosen. Then each member worked in her own section to elect the person chosen in the practice election. Of course we did all this work secretly, so that the company would not know. The workers were very careful not to let word of the project leak out.

Finally election day came. It was one day in 1972. Without knowing of the workers' secret project, the company — as before — chose candidates who had no connection with the workers' concerns and tried to compel the workers to vote for them. The workers verbally acquiesced. But inwardly they retorted, "Fool! Just wait and see what the results will be!" and felt deeply satisfied.

The election went smoothly. The workers carried out their

own promise, so everything they had planned was accomplished. The voting results were announced: of the total forty-one delegates, twenty-nine were women; and of the twenty-nine, twenty-four were precisely those chosen by the workers in the practice election.

So we were as successful as we had hoped to be. But the company side was upset. The evening after the delegate election, we gathered again with the elected twenty-four, at the Inchon Christian Society Building. This time we discussed meeting procedures and held a practice election of the chairperson. In the middle of the meeting a man suddenly opened the door and looked all around, then went away. The next morning a KCIA agent began following us, and keeping watch over me. All our members were followed by the agents, so it became difficult to hold meetings at all. We ended up meeting in the middle of the night in order to avoid their surveillance.

The twenty-four workers and I held a long discussion on whom we should choose as chairperson. Finally we selected Chu Kil Ja as our candidate. She was not included among the twenty-four, but we believed that her experience and age made her the best choice. We decided to meet Chu Kil Ja, listen to her ideas, and persuade her to be a candidate. She said that not only had there never been a woman chairperson, but that even if she were elected she would not know what to do. Since twenty-four of the forty-one delegates were our members, if Chu Kil Ja got all our votes, she would have the majority needed to be elected. We talked to her persuasively, urging her to have self-confidence and become a candidate. Finally she agreed. Together with her, we chose the executive members and helped her practice her acceptance speech.

At last the day of the delegates' conference arrived. Chu Kil Ja got twenty-four votes as we had expected and was chosen as the chairperson. The other delegates got only six or seven votes. Actually, Chu Kil Ja should have received thirty-one votes. We had arranged with a man worker to hand over seven votes to her in exchange for a position on the executive committee. If he betrayed us, we were ready to organize a women-only executive committee. But this man did not keep his promise because he could not believe Chu Kil Ja would get twenty-four votes. Actually, up to then, in the history of Dong-Il Textile Company, there had never been a case where the union chairperson got the required majority in the first vote. Moreover, it was beyond imagination that a woman could become chairperson.

The 1972 election did not just change the Dong-Il Textile union: in the whole history of labor unions in Korea, this was the first election of a woman chairperson. Having elected Chu Kil Ja, the delegates' conference rushed on to organize an all-women executive committee, composed of our members and JOC (Young Catholic Workers) members. During this meeting the delegates were surprised when Chu Kil Ja passed out. Because she was worried about trembling as she stood in front of so many people for the first time in her life, she had taken a sedative, but had overdosed. The general secretary had to preside over the remainder of the meeting. I was not able to watch the historical event because I was not permitted into the company.

This overcoming of Dong-Il Textile Union's pro-company attitude and the election of the first woman chairperson in Korea was the first fruit of my industrial mission. It was accomplished mainly through group activities and was definitely a result of responding to the workers' demands and encouraging the development of their consciousness on that basis. I grew much through this first experience.

11

Nude Demonstration

THE EXISTENCE of an all-women executive committee made the company nervous. Previously, the union could be handled by persuasion, threats, and a little money, but now it had become "noisy." That was the start of all sorts of oppressive actions against the union. Nevertheless, the union members joined in strong solidarity and struggle to cope with these difficulties.

In 1975 a new chairperson took office — again, a woman, Lee Young Sook. She was elected by an absolute majority. But the continuation of an all-women executive committee, though important for the autonomy and unity of the workers, was viewed as a threat, not only by the company but by the government as well; and in February 1976, around the time of the delegates' election, the atmosphere turned strange.

The rumor spread that the government, the KCIA, and the company were working together to eliminate Lee Young Sook and destroy the union. This rumor was proven to be true by the company's maneuverings before the 1976 election. Korea has a nationwide Consultation Committee for Labor Problems, and Inchon area also has one such area committee, consisting of a labor delegate, a company delegate, the city mayor or provincial governor, and a delegate from the KCIA. We got word through the KCIA delegate on our committee that there was a plan to arrest Lee Young Sook by setting up a false incident.

The labor delegate of the Inchon committee actively negotiated with the government side for this plan. The idea was that this delegate — a man — would persuade Lee Young Sook to withdraw as a candidate, then he would make a deal with the company to avoid extreme actions by the union. The labor delegate was a well-known and talented organizer and charismatic leader. He was also chairperson of the Automobile Workers Union, a college graduate, intellectual, and labor activist with influential links to the April 19 Revolution. He had excellent political sense and ability to solve all sorts of problems through political activity. (Later, he was eliminated by the government.)

He met Lee Young Sook and tried to persuade her: considering the expected gains and losses, it would be wise to yield temporarily this time. But Lee would not listen to him, feeling that this kind of negotiation was not right. On the contrary, she wanted to fight more strongly. She defended her stand and came to me for confirmation. I told her that this time we might lose a lot, so we had better stay calm and not raise any unnecessary trouble. Probably she was not satisfied with my advice, so she went to the Central Textile Union headquarters and discussed the matter with them. They encouraged her to fight strongly. However, the person with whom she discussed this was opposed to the above-mentioned labor delegate and was more concerned about expanding his own power to eliminate the opposition than about the Dong-Il Textile Union. As a consequence the negotiations broke down and the government side manufactured an event calculated to destroy the union.

April 3, 1976, was the day of the scheduled delegates' meeting. However, by means of a company scheme the meeting was cancelled. Koh Doo Young, the company man charged with carrying out the plan, tricked twenty delegates into going on a picnic, and thus the meeting lacked a quorum and could not be held.

On April 23, at the reopened delegates' meeting, Koh Doo Young moved for a no-confidence vote on all the executive committee members. Suddenly, however, two women delegates stood up and through personal witness criticized the company's improper actions, including bribery. They threw onto the table the money — 20,000 won — with which the company had tried to bribe them. One of the two was Koh Doo Young's sister-in-law. She had taken the money in order to expose the plot, which she now did in front of the whole meeting. The meeting scene was transformed into a crying sea of women workers; Koh Doo Young's people ran out. The remaining delegates waited for their return until ten o'clock in the evening, but they did not come, so again the meeting had to be postponed without setting a new date. Subsequently, the meeting was called twice more, but they did not show up, so it was postponed again and again.

The executive committee appealed to the Central Textile

Union for punishment of Koh and the three others who had bribed the delegates and behaved abusively toward the chairperson; and accordingly, the Central Union took disciplinary action against them. Then Koh, paying 300,000 won deposit money, appealed to the Inchon local branch of Seoul District Court for a provisional disposition suspending the disciplinary action. At the same time, with the signatures of the delegates on his side, he submitted a written request to Kyonggi Province for suspension of the Dong-Il Union executive committee's authority to call meetings. The executive committee submitted their objections, explaining about the Koh group's absence. But the Inchon branch court nevertheless approved Koh's appeal, and Koh was named by the provincial governor as the authorized meeting convener.

Koh then announced a delegates' meeting. The local union rejected this, and scheduled a report meeting with the attendance of Central Union officials. But on the evening before the meeting, at ten o'clock, the company closed the meeting place and separated Chairperson Lee Young Sook from the other members. When the members protested this, the company forcibly restrained them by mobilizing the guards and other workers.

The following day — the day of Koh's meeting — the police detained the chairperson. The Koh group met under the protection of the police and company and — having blocked all protest from the chairperson's group — elected Koh as chairperson. When the women workers heard this news they were very angry. Breaking the door and jumping from the window, they pushed through the company's blockade and ran to the union office. They shouted, "Release Chairperson Lee Young Sook!" "Koh's meeting is illegal!" "No more company oppression!" And they began a sit-down protest.

That afternoon the police released Lee Young Sook, upon which the workers ended their action and returned home. But no sooner had the workers left than the police re-arrested Lee, along with the union's general secretary, Lee Chong Kak. From the evening shift, which began at ten, the workers entered into a fast and sit-in. They resolved to go on strike if the two were not released by ten the next evening, but the police did not free them. The sit-in — a legal protest — continued for three days.

On the second day the company locked all the restrooms and shut off the water and electricity.

On the third day, the 25th of July, all traffic was diverted from the vicinity of the company. By this time the workers were lying exhausted, hot, and hungry. Outside the company fence, workers' families watched their struggle anxiously; they tried to send in water but the guards grabbed the bottles and smashed them. The most serious problem during the strike was the lack of sanitary pads. As this strike was not pre-planned, the workers were in great difficulty due to the blockade. In particular, the refusal to let them have sanitary pads made them almost frantic. Their mothers threw pads and bags of ice over the fence, but these were snatched up by company people and police.

Evening came. A bus brought riot police, armed with clubs. They surrounded the workers and began forcibly arresting them. Then an astonishing thing happened: the women workers took off their work clothes to protest the arrests. In the hot summer heat of forty degrees centigrade, the workers were mostly wearing only bras under their work clothes; so when they removed these they were half-naked. In that state they sang as loudly as they could, thinking that not even the worst policeman would lay his hands on a naked woman's body. But the police brutally arrested them, beating them with clubs, and the helpless women ran and fell, screaming and bleeding. A few women, in a last desperate act to defend the union, even took off their underpants, but the police seized them just the same and threw them into the bus. Some were beaten and dragged to the bus by their hair. Some women lay in front of the wheels of the bus to try to stop it from taking the workers. It was an agonizing scene.

In this incident seventy-two were arrested, fifty passed out from shock, more than seventy were wounded, and fourteen had to be hospitalized. Two suffered such extreme shock that they became mentally disturbed and screamed whenever they saw a man, "Police, police! I'm afraid!" One of these women was hospitalized for six months; the other was in the hospital for a year.

The next day, 300 of the workers who had escaped arrest absented themselves from work and went to the Seoul Central Textile Union to request the release of their fellow workers. As a result, the chairperson, general secretary, and all the other arrested members were released.

But the company continued its oppression and manipulation. Koh's side opened a "union office" in the company with him acting as chairperson. The executive committee appealed to the Central Union for help in solving this situation. The Central Union formed a countermeasures committee and made an apparent effort to solve the problem. The local union committee delegated its authority to the countermeasures committee and waited for the results, but was again cheated. The countermeasures committee renewed the collective agreement making the labor union pro-company and deceived the local union by reporting that negotiations were continuing.

The angry union members now had a new task: to inform the society about the injustice of the Central Union. Meanwhile the local union itself organized the "Dong-Il Textile Incident Struggle Committee" and resolved to fight hard. Fifteen of them formed a "death-defying corps," saying, "We will live together or die together." They planned a "dissection of the incident" to be held at Myongdong Cathedral, in order to explore the whole picture of oppression of labor unions since 1972 and to look for solutions.

Until then there had been not even one line in the newspapers, on TV, or on the radio about the Dong-Il Textile incident. The intelligence agents were running around in circles, trying to calm down the workers somehow and prevent the "dissection" event. They grew bloodshot-eyed trying to find me. Evidently they thought I was the "controller behind the scenes," but in fact I hadn't had any such role. I was related to Dong-Il Textile Company only from 1968 to 1972 and following that had had contact with the laborers only when they asked my help. They did everything by themselves. But the agents seemed always to believe I was pulling strings from behind. When I heard that KCIA agents were looking for me, I went to meet them by myself. They told me, "We will formally intervene to reach an agreement, so please help us," and suggested a meeting of three parties: a labor union delegate, a labor department representative, and me. I refused to participate.

Finally, instead of cancelling the "dissection" event, they agreed to have a meeting of the company president, the Central

Union's vice-chairperson, the head of the Labor Department, and labor union delegates, regarding the six demands the laborers were making.

I also attended at the agents' request, but as a third person: as a way of keeping out of the negotiations, I sat in the back and kept silent. During the meeting the laborers were very serious. They looked so stubborn even to me, insisting on their demands without yielding an inch. They wouldn't change a word of the contents of their proposals. I was deeply impressed. It was really their lives they were struggling for. The head of the Labor Department, showing signs of great frustration, looked at me as though he wanted some help. I merely responded with a helpless expression. During a recess I met with the laborers and commented that it might be good to show some flexibility.

At last the agreement was concluded, and the labor union could hold its first delegates' meeting in a year. After much suffering and struggle the April 1977 delegates' meeting elected Lee Chong Kak as the third woman chairperson of the local union, with an overwhelming majority. So Dong-Il Textile Union had given birth to three successive women chairpersons. I wept with deep emotion.

12

Dung-Throwing

FEBRUARY 21, 1978: it was the day of the union delegates' election. I got an early-morning phone call at my room inside the UIM building. Awakened from sleep, I heard an urgent voice, "Reverend, something serious has happened." It was the start of another incident at Dong-Il Textile Company. Before election day the police had come to me several times. They warned me threateningly, "This election won't be a quiet one," but I had not paid much attention. I had thought there wouldn't be much trouble, since the local union had succeeded in eliminating Koh's group. Soon I found out that the Central Textile Union and the company had prepared an elaborate plan to destroy the local union again.

At that time the country was under Emergency Measure No. 9, but even in the politically suffocating situation, the students, intellectuals, laborers, and farmers were strongly resisting the dictatorship of Park Chung Hee. The Park regime, confused by the opposition movements, devised a counterplan. Judging UIM and JOC to be the forces behind the laborers' autonomous democratic labor movement, they began systematic political oppression of these two organizations. And the Central Textile Union played the role of handmaid of the regime, leading the oppression. The head of the Central Union, Kim Young Tae, was the vicious anti-labor figure who played the main role in this "dung-throwing" event.

In advance of the delegates' election day, the Central Union carried out "education" to eliminate the democratic group by luring away Dong-Il Textile Union members. This education effort was commissioned to Kim Mi Sook (not her real name), a turncoat, former local union chairperson at Bando Company. During the education process, those who raised questions or objections became the victims of police gang violence, threats, and sexual harassment. Together with three laborers, the company was planning a most unusual strategy to oppress human rights. The local union side sensed that something strange was going on and asked the police to send four or five men to protect the orderly process of the next day's election. But election day began with screams and sounds of destruction from early in the morning. Men laborers mobilized by the company used clubs to break up the forty ballot boxes and other equipment in the union office. Meanwhile, five or six men wearing rubber gloves brought liquid dung in fire buckets. They threw it on the women workers, and with their gloved hands they plastered it on their faces and clothes. Company candidate Park Bok Rae directed a man with a dung-soaked rag, "Put it in that tramp's mouth!" The men pushed dung into the women's mouths and into their shirt fronts. A few men even chased the women to their dormitory and upturned the buckets on their heads. When some women asked the policemen beside them for help, the police shouted, "Shut up, you bitches! We'll intervene later!" About one hour later, the Labor Organizing Corps came and seized the office, with the purpose of blocking the election.

When I got word about the situation, I went to the National Council of Churches' Human Rights Committee office in Seoul. We quickly formed a countermeasures committee and published a statement urging the company not to disturb the scheduled election.

The local union members acted very calmly in the midst of this situation: they quickly cleaned up the office and made new ballot boxes to be ready for the voting at 2:00 the next morning when the early morning shift left work. Before the next day arrived, however, there was more trouble. A planned meeting to discuss the election was not permitted to start at 1:00 p.m., upon which about five hundred workers gathered and began a sit-in protest. This was broken up when they were encircled by one hundred menacing riot police.

The next day, big signs were posted on the entrance gate to the company: "Out with UIM!" "Expel outside power Lee Chong Kak!" "Catch and beat up Cho Wha Soon!" The Central Textile Union went further. Its executive committee met and agreed to consider the Dong-Il Textile Union as "problem number one" and to break up the present executive committee and remove its members' names from the union membership

list. Central Textile Union Chairperson Kim Young Tae spoke
publicly without hesitation, charging that UIM was a communist organization and that Dong-Il Textile Union was the "child
of UIM."

The indignant laborers, suffering continuously under direct
and formidable attack by the government-supported union aris-
tocracy, decided to make an appeal at the coming nationwide
Labor Day event. On March 10 at 10:00 a.m., the ceremonies
started at Changchung Stadium, with the participation of Prime
Minister Choi Kyu Ha and other related officials from the government. Everything proceeded in an orderly fashion. At around
10:30, Chung Dong Ho, the president of the National Federation of Trade Unions, was about halfway through his opening
address. At that moment, eighty women laborers from Dong-
Il Textile Company raised high the placards that they had secretly prepared beforehand and shouted, "Out with Kim Young
Tae!" "Solve the Dong-Il Textile problem!" "We cannot live,
eating dung!" "Down with labor aristocrats!" This Labor Day
event was being broadcast live over TV, so even the shouting
was heard. The event was stopped for three minutes, and the
live broadcasting was interrupted three times, for two minutes
each time. Immediately a gang — apparently a riot squad —
rushed to the scene; the women laborers were beaten up and
thrown down onto the cement floor as fast as they could reach
them. Thirty-one laborers were detained at the Seoul Central
District police station, and fifty laborers were expelled from the
company by force. Some of these participated in an evening
mass at Myongdong Cathedral. They began a fast and sit-in
from 10 o'clock in the evening at the priest's residence on the
third floor.

On the evening of March 12, more than one thousand people gathered at Dapdong Cathedral in Inchon for a Labor Day
service. I reported the Dong-Il Textile event at the service. As
I stood in front of the crowd talking, the people began to get
stirred up without my realizing it. I heard many people say that
as they listened to my words, their emotions became so intense
that they were determined to fight this injustice no matter what.
Maybe I was born with a temperament that naturally stirred up
others; that is what happened on that day. "I will live with the
laborers! My only hope is that when I die, on my tombstone will

be written, 'Cho Wha Soon lived with the laborers.' As I fast,
I will fight continuously to solve this situation!" Almost everyone in the hall was weeping, and the laborers who were there
expressed their resolve to fight with us. Together with them
I went into a fast immediately. In Myongdong Cathedral the
sit-in fast was also continuing. The fast at Dapdong Cathedral
continued for three days.

Then the government began putting pressure on the Catholic
church. In this difficult situation the Catholic leaders suggested
that we move the sit-in to another place. Even though I knew
they were very concerned about the labor issue, when they made
this request I was very upset and wept. Since we had to move,
I decided we should go to our Hwasudong office. But the cathedral was tightly surrounded by police, so to get out we had to
use a camouflage strategy. I sent the laborers out in pairs and at
the same time spread the rumor that we were ending the sit-in.
In such small numbers they had little trouble getting out. The
problem was me. I worried for some time about how to escape,
and finally made up my mind to disguise myself as a Catholic
sister. I asked the priest's and sisters' help to borrow a nun's
robe, because according to Catholic law, they cannot give their
clothes away to anyone. I had put them into a difficult situation. Finally, however they brought me a sister's clothing. I put
it on, changed my glasses, and went out with two sisters and a
priest, riding in the priest's car to Hwasudong. When I got off
in front of my office the police looked at me sharply, but since
four of us were together I was not suspected. Through a side
door I got into my office. There the laborers were waiting for
me. As they saw me in the sister's garb they burst into cheers
and applause. Including the staff, sixty-seven entered the fast
again without setting any ending date.

During this time we had incidents of intrusion by gangs, attempts at appeasement through the workers' parents, and threats
from the police, but — disconnected from the outside — we
continued the sit-in for thirteen days. After our move to Hwasudong, various groups began to try to solve the Dong-Il Textile
problem. People from various fields came together to form an
"urgent countermeasures committee on the Dong-Il Textile incident." This committee negotiated with high government officials and got their promise that the Dong-Il Textile situation

would be restored to the state it had been in before the February 22 delegates' election. Upon receiving the promise, the 111 laborers fasting at Myongdong Cathedral in Seoul and at the Hwasudong office in Inchon dispersed their sit-in. But the laborers were cheated again. Those who came back to work were threatened and ordered to write a memo promising not to make any more trouble. At the same time, the false propaganda about UIM was becoming more vicious.

Not only that but the company, reasoning that the striking laborers had caused vast damage to the company and that the workers had been absent without notice for three days, formally requested a permit from the Kyonggi Province Labor Committee that would exempt it from giving the required prior notice when discharging workers. The labor committee obliged, and on April 1 the company discharged 124 laborers in a mass firing. Subsequently the Central Textile Union made a blacklist of the 124 and sent it around to all the companies in Korea.

I travelled all over the country, giving speeches and holding prayer meetings, to raise public opinion and build solidarity among conscientious people regarding the laborers' situation. The fired laborers struggled for years to be rehired; in fact, their problem continued up to the "1984 Blacklist Struggle."

Every year since 1972, the Dong-Il Textile Union elections were broken up. In the first place this was caused by the Park regime's vicious political oppression and the deliberate effort of the Korean Federation of Trade Unions to destroy democratic labor unions. The second factor was the authorities' oppression of UIM, the laborers' friend. But in spite of the terrible risks, the Dong-Il Textile laborers continued to fight, and through their struggle their political consciousness was raised. Going beyond the economic issue or a simple demand for higher wages, the Dong-Il Textile Union struggle has a strong political character, as a broad struggle against company and government power that obstructs the democratic activity of labor unions. Maybe that's why the company and government oppressed it more and more. One high official complained he could never have a good night's sleep because of the Dong-Il Textile Union.

On September 22, 1978, at a prayer meeting for the Dong-Il union in the Christian Building auditorium, Seoul, the fired Dong-Il laborers presented a play about the dung incident. Actors and audience alike were swept away in a sea of anger and tears. When the drama was ended it was naturally followed by an overnight sit-in, with the workers shouting, "Secure the three rights of labor! Abolish the Yushin Constitution! Step down, Park regime!" In the middle of this protest, the riot police suddenly attacked and the auditorium became a screaming hell. Police clubs were thrashing, people were thrown out the door — the terrible disturbance was beyond imagination. In this incident forty laborers and others were arrested, interrogated, and imprisoned. I was interrogated for nineteen days.

13

Bando Company Struggle

INCHON UIM WAS FOCUSING ON THE ISSUE of how to raise the quality of its group activities, after evaluation of their progress during the early 1970s. One of these activities — the educational program of the women workers' group — was the stimulus for Bando Company laborers to start their own organizational activity and struggle.

It may be said that the leading actors in Korea's economic development during the 1970s were mostly the women workers in the textile, electronics, sewing, and wigmaking industries, which produced the main articles for export. The government and business enterprises used women's unequal sexual status to exploit their labor, with the aim of obtaining foreign currency. The situation at Bupyong Export Industrial Complex was no exception.

The Bupyong program, called "Bupyong Women Leaders Training," started on December 8, 1973, and was held twice a month for three months. It was planned and led by just two persons, Choi Young Hee and me, with the detailed plan and procedure a secret even from the other staff. What made this program different from other group activities at the center was that it was designed to educate leaders of the labor movement. The course had three steps: first, to raise the ability to make social scientific analysis of social issues: second, to explore how the laborers were currently working to solve labor problems; third, to practice actual involvement in dealing with the labor situation. The trainees were gathered secretly, mostly through person-to-person contacts by members of UIM. As usual, the political situation at that time also was very tight, so we had to do everything in secret.

There were only eight members who gathered at that time, from the Bando Company factory and three other companies. It was as a result of this training that the Bando incident took place. The Bando members, whether by chance or not, had some disposition for movement and sincerely carried out their task. But those who were from the other three companies dropped out in the early stages for personal reasons or failed to initiate any movement in their factories. Only the Bando members succeeded.

One laborer from Bando was Kim Mi Sook. She seemed to have talent for movement. She was quick to understand and digested new ideas immediately and embodied them in her life. She had leadership and the know-how to plan things and make her fellow workers trust her, even though she had never been involved in the labor movement before or had any education on labor issues. She was a treasure discovered in the "Bupyong district women leaders' training." Together with Kim Mi Sook we prepared for organizing and struggle in the Bando Company.

The only systematic organizational structure in our country to fight and negotiate with a company in order to claim and realize workers' rights is the labor union. Therefore the organization of labor unions is very important. In the Bando case this had to start with the fundamental problem of how to form a labor union. After the women leaders' training, we moved to the practical organizing task and discussed how to plan our basic strategy. The issue was whether we should first organize the labor union and then fight for it, or first raise a fight over a common issue in the working field and then, on its basis, organize the union.

Choi Young Hee and I chose the latter. This was a decision based on our past experience of organizing and struggle. When we had used the method of organizing the union first, the priority had to be to manage the union and problems with the company, so that relations among the members weakened and complaints arose between the union management and members. But through the method of fighting first, solidarity was formed naturally and a strong union could be organized from the beginning. Therefore, the first fight should include all the workers in fellowship and must be carried out successfully. Everything should be exact and accurate.

In Bando company we used a three-step organizing method. It is the best method by which to establish a sound position

for the leader and to proceed completely without the knowledge of the company. During the women leaders' training we
helped Kim Mi Sook to meet influential workers in every field
of the Bando Company. After the education was completed,
Kim started group meetings with them and prepared to have
conscientization training for the group. They were fourteen in
number, and this increased to twenty-six. In contrast to the education program in which Kim Mi Sook had participated, we had
this group operate by themselves. Except for professional assistance from the staff, we made sure everything was authentically
carried out through Kim Mi Sook by consulting and sending
messages.

Then, during this period, we asked Kim to choose three persons in whom she could confide and who could work together.
Thus there was formed a team of four with Kim as leader. This
team, with the staff's suggestions and advice, planned their goals
and strategy through their own discussions and decisions. This
took one month; then came the authentic action, the strike.

In this phase Choi Young Hee was more active than I. Choi
was a young woman, under thirty, a graduate of Ewha University's department of sociology. She had led the student movement at Ewha and is remembered as an immortal figure. I liked
her charming style — long, straight hair and a beautiful slim,
tall figure — and respected her passion and excellent movement
sense. It was the principle of Inchon UIM to respect the autonomy of the workers and to proceed with activities on this basis,
and she excelled in this.

The Bando workers made the unanimous decision to strike,
setting the date as February 26, 1974. They raised an activities
fund from their small wages, contributing 1,000 won each, and
found a printing shop to print their letter of appeal. Kim Mi
Sook, who had a talent for writing, wrote a beautiful letter. They
decided Kim would be the first striker; if she got arrested, the
second striker would take over, then the third and fourth. All
twenty-six had their role to play. Those six who were responsible
for public relations decided not to go to work but to go directly
to the newspapers.

On February 25, they put part of the letters (with maps telling
where to meet) in a sack for the workers to pick up on their way
out from work. The rest they distributed to each room in the

dormitory. Kim Mi Sook went around to each room, explaining the purpose of the strike and appealing for unity. She told them, "I will be responsible for everything." Everybody believed her and promised to meet at the place shown on the map, at 8:20 a.m. the next day.

It was an exciting night. Thinking of all the sorrows they had suffered and the strike that would happen tomorrow, under the blankets some were crying, some breathless, some overflowing with joy, some trembling with fear.

The next morning the workers in the dormitory ate breakfast in the dining hall just like on any ordinary day; then they changed into their working clothes and waited for the appointed time of 8:20. Those who were coming from their homes also changed into working clothes and waited for the dormitory workers to come out all together — this was the agreed sign. Finally the dormitory workers appeared and within five minutes all the workers had gathered in the second floor handwork room and begun to barricade the entrance. Handing over the list of prepared slogans, white paper, and magic markers, we asked those section leaders who were comparatively uninvolved to write the slogans to be put on the walls or poles. This was done purposely to get them more involved and lead their section members in raising the will to fight.

As planned, the stronger section members stood around the periphery and the weaker section members in the middle. The action began with the responsible leaders creating the atmosphere. None of the more than 1,400 workers had told anybody about the strike, even though the superintendent of the dormitory was right next door. The many who came to work from their homes also kept the plan secret, though they mingled with the office workers and managers on their way to the company. This shows how deep their resentment was: it was manifested in a powerful unity.

As soon as the demonstration started, the company management realized what was happening and there was an uproar. They immediately sent messages to the main company and main compound; and all the office workers and guards surrounded the women laborers and tried by persuasion and threats to break up their protest, but it was no use. The workers presented the following six demands:

1. A 60 percent salary raise.

2. Punishment of violence by company staff.

3. Improvement of working conditions and dormitory facilities.

4. Establishment of work rules.

5. Abolition of forced overtime work.

6. Whatever sacrifice we must make for this just struggle, we will continue to fight to the end. We demand a clear and public promise from company president Ku Ja Seung, on the above demands.

These demands were an expression of the deep resentment all the Bando workers felt toward the company.

The starting salary at that time was 153 won a day, while a technician with five years' experience got only 510 won a day. This was a murderously low income. Moreover, overtime work was always required, and often overnight work. The managers customarily beat the workers, and, as an oil-saving measure, there was no heat in the dormitory. This big Korean enterprise with such unimaginably bad working conditions and wages for its 1,400 workers was an acclaimed export company.

The strike was heating up, with a speech by Kim Mi Sook, the reading of the appeal letter, and the shouting of slogans. No amount of persuasion by the company manager, the chairperson of the board of directors from the main company compound, the strike manager of the Central Textile Union, or the police could cool down the heat. Kim Mi Sook's voice trembled with suffering and sadness and screamed with righteous anger. The voices of the workers also trembled as they shouted slogans and sang together. Always keeping proper order, they called for the company to accept their demands. Meanwhile, the police broke the window, came into the room, and began to pull out the workers. But because the workers had gone into a scrum circle formation with the leader in the middle, the police could not reach her. Whenever the police made any threatening comment, the workers spontaneously yelled together, "Wooooooo!" to drown out the sound. They demanded to meet the company president.

The chief of negotiations from the Central Textile Union began to speak soothingly, "Dear workers! Why are you acting like this? We can solve this kind of problem through the labor union. Now, this strike is illegal. You must disperse right away, then organize a labor union." The workers shouted, "You are the same as the others! We will no longer be deceived! Bring the president now!"

The strike continued till 10 o'clock at night. After agreement was reached between the company and the workers' delegates, they broke up. The negotiation team had five delegates from each side with the added presence of the police. The workers' demands were not achieved 100 percent, but overall they were successful. Even the condition "This event will not be investigated" was accepted, and the strike ended cleanly without anyone being fired. Through this event the workers realized directly that united they could overcome any kind of power.

The organizing assembly for the labor union was set for March 5. It was the general sentiment that Kim Mi Sook should be elected as chairperson of the local union. Then the atmosphere in the company became strange. Actually the company did not want Kim to run for chairperson and therefore was plotting to manipulate the process. Their scenario was to manufacture a company-controlled union by bribing the person they had in mind to elect. Kim Mi Sook and her group found out the secret and devised a counterplan.

It was March 5. There was not just one strange thing but several at the organizing assembly. The election of the nominating committee was strange, and so was the attitude of the assembly moderator (the disputes manager from the Central Textile Union). As the intentions of the company became increasingly clearer in the process of the assembly, there was increasing tension on the floor. When the moderator said, "A woman cannot be chairperson of a local union," the workers began to become agitated. At that moment one woman worker stood up, crying, and shouted out the facts of the company's plot. "Dear fellow workers, I am sorry. I was wrong. The company has already bribed several men and women to make a company union according to their scenario. I told them I would okay whatever the company wanted me to do. The Central Union's disputes manager told me to pretend I did not know anything."

The furious workers stood up all together and shouted, "Kill the disputes manager!" Some cried and some passed out, they were so indignant over having been deceived and deceived again. Looking at a fellow worker lying unconscious with froth at her lips, another worker pounded her chest and wailed, "Why are they doing this to us?" The floor became a flood of tears. Then Kim Mi Sook took the microphone. "Friends, the company and Central Union have deceived us. The agreement we reached after the fight of the 26th has gone down the drain. Let us start a sit-in demonstration to demand the signing of the six articles without any conditions and the firing of the Central Union disputes manager." With no dissent, they immediately went into a sit-in. The workers' trust in Kim Mi Sook was marvelous. Even in the midst of crying and shouting confusion, if Kim came out in front they became calm, listened to whatever she suggested, and followed the decision.

The sit-in continued overnight to early morning. At 7:30 a.m., fifty plainclothes police officers, who were called by the company from Bupyong police station, together with company office workers and guards, came and surrounded the women workers. They held clubs in their hands. The workers, leaning against each other, tired from hunger, cold, and a sleepless night, sensed the situation, but they did not have time to protest and were beaten up mercilessly. Most of them were already in a physically weak condition. When they were beaten, some passed out, some fell down, some clung to the police, as suddenly the place became chaos. Holding fellow workers who had fallen, escaping from clubs, and running away — they were frantic. Some were bleeding; some were caught by the hair and dragged by the police.

The police and company men were wild-eyed trying to find the leaders. They checked every room and found one leader hidden in a cabinet. Hundreds of workers sneaked outside to escape but had to fight with the guards at the front gate. Kim Mi Sook ran up to the top of the building. The roof was flat and there was no place to hide. The police were following just behind her. At that moment she jumped to the next building. It was an unthinkable act, but she was desperate to escape and let the world know the facts. The distance between the buildings was quite wide, nearly impossible to jump, and there was a high-voltage electric line between them. The slate roof of the next building was broken when she jumped. Her leg was injured and she was immediately grabbed. Twenty-one workers were arrested and the rest of them again held a strike in the company for their release.

The twenty-one arrested workers were investigated about the sit-in on that day, the February 26 strike, their connections with UIM, their connections with Rev. Cho, etc. Until then the connection with UIM had not been disclosed. Kim Mi Sook and four other core members denied everything when questioned, especially about any connection with UIM. One interrogator, waving the appeal letter that Kim had written, chided her, "Hey, who will believe you wrote this? Didn't you only graduate from grade school? An uneducated person like you writing a letter like this — it just doesn't make sense. There must be somebody who was controlling you. Quickly confess the truth!"

Kim Mi Sook asked him for a pen and paper, put the paper on the desk, and told him, "If you cannot believe me, then give me any topic to write on and I will write here and now and show you directly." The interrogators believed Kim Mi Sook due to her frank and clever answers during the interrogation. A person like her, they became convinced, could do everything without outside control. That evening they promised to release all the workers. The moment they were coming out of the police station, the telephone rang. One interrogator held the phone, his face hardened, then he shouted, "Just one moment! Hold them!" Everybody was stunned, wondering what was going on. The police soon released all but Kim and the four core members. They were to interrogate them again. The content of the phone message had been that the leaders were deeply involved in UIM.

Interrogation had been conducted not only of the twenty-one arrested but also of those who were striking at the company. From one of these the police found out the involvement of UIM. The worker was the sister of a core member. She innocently told about a meeting her sister had had and her plans that she had accidentally overheard.

This unexpected turn of events had thrown everything wide open. The interrogators were enraged about having been deceived. They beat up the workers very badly, then sent them to the Korean Central Intelligence Agency. Delivered over to the Namsan KCIA headquarters, the leaders told the investigators everything during several days of torture and guided questioning. Finally they even told them what I had said once, "When things go wrong, do not involve Choi Young Hee. Attribute everything to me. It is all right because I am a minister, but she is a graduate of university, so she might be charged as a communist. In our country anything against the government is imputed to communism." Through the process of the KCIA's counter-education, the workers now became suspicious of us; we might be communists.

Probably because of that, they did not come to us after their release. We were anxious to know what was going on, but we waited in vain. Choi Young Hee was so concerned and worried about them that she decided to go to a place where she thought they might come. One of the four, Chang Hyon Ja, was a Catholic, so we went to visit every Catholic cathedral in Bupyong. Finally, our guess turned out right, and we found her. Choi Young Hee happily shouted, "Hyon Ja!" Chang Hyon Ja turned around, but when she saw who was calling her, she looked terrified and ran away. Her expression was just like she had seen a snake. Later we heard that she had thought, "Isn't she a communist?" Facing such an unexpected rejection, Choi Young Hee was heartbroken and wept.

The UIM staff discussed how to restore our relationship with the workers. Eventually we decided to ask the male chairperson of the union of a local company, who was one of our members, to arrange a meeting with them. He successfully persuaded them and we met them again. We had dinner together with the four leaders and shared our thoughts. We found out what had happened meanwhile, and the leaders wept with deep emotion. Even though they had been interrogated by the KCIA, they had not been fired and came to work regularly. In spite of the company's obstruction they had organized the labor union successfully. Kim Mi Sook was elected chairperson with unanimous support, and with the other three formed a solid executive committee of only women.

Later on they stopped contacts with us and managed the labor union activities by themselves. We also did not feel the necessity to have regular connections. For one thing, the distance between Inchon and Bupyong was too great. But even more than that, we absolutely trusted the excellent leadership of their executive committee.

14

Betrayal

FOLLOWING THE BANDO INCIDENT, Kim Mi Sook turned traitor
to the union. With her excellent organizing and leadership ability, she played the role of spy, handing over our secret information to the KCIA. Now I think that when the laborers were
released from interrogation, she and the KCIA had made some
kind of bargain; but I still have no definite evidence of this. Mi
Sook used to stop by our Inchon office once in a while to greet
us. After the labor union was organized we did not have such
close relations as before. When she came by, I would greet her
simply, "How are you? Is everything okay? Is the union doing
all right?" She always answered, "Yes, everything is fine. Nothing special is happening. Don't worry, Reverend." So I thought
they had no problems; but I found out later that they did.

It was purely by accident that I found out that Mi Sook
was sending information about us to the KCIA. We were engaged in a program for workers after we had established the
Kwangya (wilderness) Church. The title was "Education for
Sunday School Teachers"; Hwang Young Hwan, a student from
Korea University, and I, as a team of three, were leading the
program. This included the history of Sunday schools, teachers'
education, and also — because most of the group were workers — education on labor issues. Actually it was mainly labor
education. Then one day during the program, the Korea University student was taken by the KCIA, who said he was involved in
the labor issue, and that his teaching during the education was
subversive. But the real intention of the KCIA was to find a
clue from our activity that would enable them to crush all UIM
activities as "operations by impure forces." In any event, in
order to investigate the Korea University student's comments,
the KCIA insisted it had to question the workers who were in
the education program.

Because of this incident the education had stopped and its

members had hidden. The police were looking for one of the core members when it became known that Kim Mi Sook was co-operating in the search. There happened to be a person, closely related to us, who was stationed at Bupyong police station in the defense corps. During the incident he overheard a KCIA agent talking on the phone: "Is that Mi Sook? You've got to help me meet that worker I asked you to contact, no matter what kind of method you use. Understand?" Actually, at that time Kim was coming to Kwangya Church. When we heard this report we were speechless. We now realized that she was spying for the KCIA. I did not want to believe it, but I remembered that her attitude and actions had been somewhat uneasy for some time.

In a few days I saw the reality with my own eyes. The worker who was wanted by the police was being kept well-hidden. But she could not continue running forever because it was so tiring. I decided to take her to the police station. I thought I might be allowed to sit with her during the investigation and bring her out with me. I called the police and told them if this condi-tion were accepted I would take her. The chief of the station accepted, so we went. The interrogation took place in a small room beside the information department office. I was bored sit-ting in the room and came out into the office. I walked around, leafed through a book on the table, then saw something covered by a piece of paper on the next desk. Without thinking, I lifted the paper, and what I saw written there made me gasp: "Infor-mation offered by Kim Mi Sook." I was trembling. There were other papers, too, apparently being used to interrogate the Ko-rea University student. Most of them were designed to find out the workers' links with me and UIM. And I was sure they were based on information from Kim.

I was heart-stricken over Mi Sook's having become such a person. Meanwhile, her betrayal was also being revealed through the labor union activities. It was the season of wage raises, and she had deceived the union members and was nego-tiating secretly with the company. The labor union and company were currently in sharp confrontation over the wage issue, hav-ing great difficulty in agreeing on the new salary level. So the labor union side decided to hold a hunger strike. The executive committee — including the chairperson, Kim — set up every-thing, the plan, dates, and detailed process. Then, just before

"D-day," one of the core members was looking for some urgently needed documents. She searched everywhere except the chairperson's drawer, which was locked. Kim was out and there was no key to open it. Finally she opened the drawer by another method. She was lifting this and that, trying to find the papers she needed, when she uncovered a strange document. It was a new salary contract, already signed by both the company president and Kim Mi Sook. She was breathless with shock. The company and chairperson had already finished the negotiations secretly, without the union members' knowledge. Chairperson Kim had played a double role. The hunger strike for a wage raise was abandoned.

After several such incidents, the executive committee members could no longer trust the chairperson. They came to me to discuss the matter, and I again became involved with the Bando union. I was in agony over the problem of firing Kim and forming a new executive committee, which the members were demanding. My heart ached when I thought of Kim. But I knew it was not right to leave the situation as it was. I decided to try to get her fired as chairperson and expelled from the labor union, and then to form a new executive committee. For that project we began members' education in our UIM center, as well as in their rented room. Sometimes ten members came, and sometimes only two. We continued nearly up to the date of the next delegates' assembly, until all the members had taken part in my education course at least once. Kim Mi Sook knew this education was going on, and though she didn't say anything, she was not happy about it.

One day, just before the assembly, I called Kim to come to my office. I had to tell her I knew about her betrayal and her espionage activities. She came together with the general secretary. I suggested that the general secretary leave so that Kim and I could talk privately, but Kim rejected this suggestion. She probably sensed that I wanted to talk about the union. I told her, "This is not a matter of whether you are the right one to be chairperson; it is a very important matter concerning your personal life. It would be better to have a private talk, just the two of us." But she again refused. She had no idea I knew about her informant's role.

At last, in front of the general secretary, I told her all I had heard and seen. Then I said very quietly, "After all this, what do you expect me to think of you? Now I cannot trust you. You are not the same Kim Mi Sook I knew before. If I had heard it only from others I could reconsider, but I have seen it with my own eyes. Whatever excuse you give me I cannot trust you." Kim was shocked and started to explain herself, but I stopped her short, "I do not trust you now." She sat quietly for a while and then left. That was our final parting.

I worked to have a new person elected as union chairperson. As a result, at the next assembly, Kim Mi Sook had to retire upon the no-confidence vote of the members. Chang Hyon Ja became the new chairperson, and she formed a new executive committee.

After returning to the position of ordinary factory worker, Kim Mi Sook became active in anti-union activity and spread bad rumors about UIM among the movement people. She accused UIM of being "the place where a person is cultivated and then when she is no longer useful she is devoured." Those who did not know the details believed what she said and made trouble over her issue. In various ways, because of Kim Mi Sook, the Bando situation was in confusion. Later on Kim was selected by the Central Textile Union to act as chairperson of its women's division. The Bando problem was thus settled for a while.

Kim Mi Sook's betrayal was a shocking event for me. I reflected on my judgment regarding movement leaders' abilities. Now I realize that she was a clever and excellent organizer and leader, but basically she had the ambition to become a star, and this led her easily to turn traitor. Her activity had started not out of deep conviction in the movement, but rather for the realization of her ambition. Therefore, when she faced the temptation to fulfill that ambition, she quickly betrayed the movement.

I must add one thing more about Kim. From 1978 to 1980 our government manipulated the mass media in order to try to destroy UIM as an "impure, procommunist organization." At the same time she was ordered to appear on a TV program of government propaganda criticizing UIM and me. But she refused, saying, "I am not that far degraded." Later I heard that she had been pressured and threatened at a very difficult time, but had still rejected the TV proposal.

Even though she and I are separated, I cannot forget her, and for Kim also, I will always be an unforgettable person in her life.

Ψ

Subsequently the Bando union, with its well-organized power and fighting ability, carried on a strong struggle with the company. The government noticed the Bando labor union and repressed it systematically. At that time the Dong-Il Textile Union was almost broken; there were rumors that the next would be Bando, and after Bando would be Wonpoong. Later these rumors became fact.

I was involved in Bando continuously. I judged that the Bando union was sure to be destroyed by government power. I told the union members that it was their moral duty to fight. I wanted to see public opinion raised through the event of Bando's destruction, which was the object of maneuvers by the government, the KCIA, and the company. There was no escape from destruction. But the executive committee did not accept my idea. They wanted to avoid an incident and try to keep the union alive.

Later I heard that they consulted with various others on the problem. There were basically two conflicting strategies: one, to fight hard under the assumption that the union would be destroyed anyway; and the other, to protect the continued existence of the union. Staffer Shin from the Christian Academy joined me in the first opinion, while Park Yong Sok from Wonpoong, a representative of the Central Textile Union, and JOC wanted to continue. The executive committee chose the second strategy.

On March 13, 1981, however, the whole matter was concluded upon the decision by Lucky Business Group to close down Bando Company. So the Bando union came to an end. Of course the Bando workers regretted their strategy, but it was too late. Most outsiders do not know what happened to the Bando union, because it did not become a publicized incident.

Since then the unemployed workers have operated an "alley tea room" as a kind of credit union, staying around the area to meet one another and carry on educational and fellowship activities.

15

First Imprisonment

ON THE MORNING OF MAY 15, 1974, the police broke into my house and I was arrested for the first time. But I was not really surprised; I was expecting it. Of course, I did not know the exact reason for the arrest, but there was at the time an ongoing investigation of a small incident connected with me. The content of my sermon at a worship service was the problem: there were hints that my thinking was "impure." So the people who had heard my sermon were interrogated.

The problem sermon was preached on April 28, 1974, at a picnic service for UIM member workers. The theme was "Search for the Kingdom and for Righteousness." That day there were workers from Bando Company participating in the worship service with us who hadn't attended for some time. I remembered their suffering during the strike and repented of my failure to live according to my words. We had planned to have the service all together, but because of rain we were divided into two bungalows. Forty-five of us gathered in our bungalow for worship. I preached according to my sermon title, "Our reality is completely the opposite of the justice of God. In our society, if we say 'white' when we see white or 'black' when we see black, we will be arrested. Now many students and ministers are suffering for this reason. We as workers should not be afraid of arrest, but must fight against the injustices in our working places."

There must have been a spy from the KCIA in the group. The next day all the workers who had been at the picnic were

detained and interrogated, mostly in connection with my sermon. Under these circumstances, I was sure they would come
to take the preacher herself.

The first place I was taken was the basement of the Kyonggi
Province KCIA center at Kansokdong, Inchon. It was the first
time in my life I had been taken to such a place and I was scared.
Remembering the stories of those who had experienced interrogation and terrible torture, I had goose-bumps all over my body.
Furthermore, the political situation had hardened. Since 1972,
when the Park regime had promulgated the Yushin Constitution,
the anti-Yushin movement had continued without letup. Particularly active at that time was the signature campaign appealing
for amendment of the Yushin Constitution. In reaction to this,
on January 8, 1974, the authorities announced Emergency Decree No. 1, and beginning with Chang Jun Ha and Paik Ki Wan,
many persons including ministers and university students were
taken to the military court for violation of the emergency decree. By the time Emergency Decree No. 4 was promulgated
on April 3, the provisions on the punishment of violations had
been greatly reinforced. For instance, in case of violation of
E.D. No. 1, the maximum penalty was fifteen years' imprisonment. Now, in case of E.D. No. 4, the minimum was fifteen
years and the maximum penalty was death. Already many students and intellectuals had been arrested for violation of E.D.
No. 4. When I thought of spending fifteen years in prison I was
afraid.

As soon as we reached the basement interrogation room, I
was told to sit in a chair, whereupon three interrogators came
and began abusing me with terrible, ugly language, mostly connected with sex. It seemed to me they were trying to use my
identity as a virgin and member of the clergy to make me feel
so ashamed that I would submit under their abuse. In fact I felt
unbearably ashamed and scared. My body trembled with fear
and my mind couldn't focus. I closed my eyes. This time they
cursed at me and demanded that I open my eyes. I felt my body
shrinking from the fear.

Then suddenly two things vividly came to my fear-filled
mind. One was, "When they bring you to be tried..., do not
be worried about how you will defend yourself, or what you
will say. For the Holy Spirit will teach you at that time what

you should say" (Luke 12:11–12). I seemed to hear Jesus' voice clearly. The other was a joke I used to use when I talked to the workers about all humans being equal. "You go to the toilet, right? Don't all human beings go to the toilet just the same? Who is the most scary person to you? The company president? He goes to the toilet. Me? I go to the toilet, the same as you all. Minister or president — all are the same as you. Whoever they are, human beings are all equal. You should not be afraid of anyone, because everybody is the same human being who eats rice and goes to the toilet." I remembered how the workers had laughed together.

I smiled quietly. Feeling some release from my fear I asked myself, "Why am I trembling like this? What am I afraid of? How can one living as a servant called by the Lord be shaking like this? Didn't Jesus tell us the Holy Spirit would speak for us when we stand in court because of him?" I was ashamed but at the same time I found self-confidence and composure. I suddenly felt relaxed. It did not matter if I was imprisoned for fifteen years, or even if I got the death penalty. "This one life I will live for the Lord though I live, die for the Lord though I die...." My attitude toward the interrogators had turned 180 degrees. I even felt the calling to use that moment to let them know the will and life of the Lord.

"You say I am agitating the workers. If so, then Jesus can also be called a rabble-rouser. He took the side of the oppressed. This means that the oppressed are precious beings created in the image of God. Jesus urged them to wake up from their oppressed thinking and find their own image; that was his teaching. It seems you are calling this rabble-rousing, but if that is so, then Jesus was a rabble-rouser and I — who am trying to resemble him — am also a rabble-rouser. What is wrong with that kind of agitating?"

The interrogators were listening quietly as if absorbed by my new firm attitude, but suddenly shouted, "What? Where do you think you are? Are you preaching to us? Can you answer when questioned?" "Ha, ha, I know where I am — the KCIA interrogation room," I laughed. Then one of the interrogators responded, "Well! I've been working as an interrogator for thirty years, but it's my first time to meet such a person!"

From then on they seemed to have given up trying to dom-

inate me by shouting me down, and their questioning became
very polite. The interrogation continued until the next morning. They questioned me about my childhood and about why I
had become involved in UIM. I explained fully about my life.
Rather than being interrogated, I was telling my story and the
workers' story and at times they seemed very moved.

On the next day their attitude toward me changed even further. One of the interrogators said he had told his wife he was
investigating a minister, and she had warned him, "If you do not
treat a minister well then you will be in big trouble, so please
be careful." In contrast to the previous day, he brought me
plenty of food and behaved very tenderly toward me. The first
night I had been given only one blanket, but after I had gone
to bed on the second night, one of the interrogators sneaked in
with a second blanket and put it over me. After a while the second interrogator came and covered me with yet another blanket.
And — believe it or not — a little later the third one came in
very quietly and covered me again. The three of them had done
this secretly, in violation of regulations. With the four blankets
I was warm and slept very comfortably.

I spent four days there, and then was transferred to the central KCIA headquarters. There the interrogation was not on
the content of my sermon, but concentrated on my thinking
and whether I had any connections with the National Federation of Democratic Youth and Students (NFDYS) incident in
April. They had the idea that I had "bought" the workers and
agitated them to raise social unrest. The reason they had detained me, in fact, was not related specifically to my sermon as
such, but they had seized upon certain "clues" from it and —
based on political motives — were intent on blocking my activities. "Buying and agitating the workers" referred to my involvement in the Bando strike and the process of organizing the labor
union. They focused consistently on the point that I had bought
the workers with money and stirred them up. They could not
seem to understand that the workers acted independently, on
their own convictions and out of their own awareness. It did
not make sense to them that without concrete personal benefit
these young women had undertaken such risky action. I realized that our value systems were completely different. I could
only tell them that the total amount of money I had spent on

the workers was the 4,000 won I had contributed toward their lunch of noodles one day. In fact, the workers had spent more than that on me, so there was no basis for the accusation.

As for my alleged connections with the NFDYS demonstrations, there were none, so in spite of their long, stubborn tracing they could not find a thing. Regardless of that, however, after this second four-day interrogation period, I was moved to Seodaemoon Prison for violation of Emergency Decree No. 4.

My cell was the very same one where high-school girl patriot Yu Kwan Sun was detained during the March 1st Movement. Maybe because of its age, it smelled terrible, and I had a hard time with the bugs. I was imprisoned there for three months. I was allowed no meetings with anyone, not even my family. I was even prohibited from doing physical exercise. I just sat in the room for three months. I was given half a teakettle of water each day, with which I had to wash my dishes and bathe. Using all my wisdom to conserve that small amount of water, I managed to bathe regularly.

Around that time, thirty-four persons had been arrested in the Ulleungdo espionage case. The alleged chief of the spies, a woman, was right in the next cell. I was anxious to see her face, to know what kind of woman she was. She also wanted to see me. But because she also was prohibited from meeting her family and going out for exercise, we could not meet each other. Then one day I got clever. There was a square hole in the door for food and water. I managed to get my head halfway through the hole, and I saw her. The term "spy" did not seem to fit. She was very beautiful and looked gentle and kind. I was enjoying talking with her, lying with my face in the hole, when suddenly I was seen by the guard. Afraid of what might happen, I retreated and covered myself with my blanket, and lay there shaking. The guard came and shouted, "If you ever do that again, I will put your face in the hole all day long!" The guards did not seem to understand why I had done such a thing. I did not act like a prisoner; I was always dignified but at the same time joking and cheerful.

One day, one of the guards came and asked, "Are you really a woman minister?" "Why do you ask?" "That woman guard and man guard over there had a big fight. The woman told the man that you are a minister, and he said, 'Where in the world is there such a thing as a woman minister? Don't lie!' The woman was angry and fought with him. So I came to find out. Are you a real minister?" "Of course I am a real minister." He looked surprised, then went back to the others. I must have been the subject of conversation.

Prison life was hard and painful, but I was able to adjust after a while. On August 8, I was called by the military court prosecutor, who surprisingly told me, "You are free today by suspension of indictment!" Soon my mission department's general secretary came and wrote a formal apology note and I was freed on that very day. I did not know why I had suddenly been released. Later I found that many women's organizations had sent word abroad about my imprisonment, and as a result many messages came, pressuring the government to release me.

After my release I remembered my joking proposal to Interrogator Lee, "When I am out, I will invite you on a date." So I called him by phone to say I would like to invite him for lunch. But his voice over the phone was extremely weak. "Ah, Rev. Cho? Thank you for remembering me. Well, I am not in good health. Probably I was punished for sending you to prison. I have been sick and in the hospital since then; I came home just a few days ago and cannot eat yet." "That's too bad. I will pray for your quick recovery." Some time later I met one of the other interrogators in Inchon, and asked about Lee. He told me that Lee had died.

In the interrogator's world they say there is a jinx on anyone who interrogates a minister.

16

Second Imprisonment

MY SECOND IMPRISONMENT, in November 1978, happened somewhat absurdly. The direct reason was that the content of one of my lectures was deemed "subversive." I was always in trouble, because from the moment I stood on a platform to speak or preach, it seemed I could not help being "agitative."

In 1978, Dong-Il Textile Company had fired 124 workers en masse, according to the joint plan of the company and the Central Textile Union, which was a puppet of the government. This resulted in an endless fight by the workers for reinstatement. These fired workers travelled to Pusan to campaign against Kim Young Tae, the chairperson of the Central Textile Union, who was running for election as a delegate to the "People's Autonomous Assembly for Unification." In Pusan, the workers distributed printed materials exposing Kim Young Tae's anti-worker activities and thereby arguing that he was not qualified to hold a leadership position in such a unification assembly. Seven of these workers were forthwith arrested on suspicion of violation of the election law concerning the "People's Assembly." They were all detained in Pusan Prison.

On November 5, I went to Pusan to send in some "custody money" to the detained workers.* I wanted to meet them but only family members were allowed visits, so I just deposited the money. As it was already evening, I thought I would look around Pusan and postpone my return to Inchon till next morning. I was walking around downtown when I saw a poster in front of the train station announcing a "Catholic-Protestant Autumn Lecture," being held at the Pusan YMCA. Thinking this would be interesting, I decided to attend. As I was entering the meeting place, somebody greeted me in a glad voice. I turned around

*A custom in Korea, allowing prisoners to buy a little extra food to supplement the inadequate supply provided.

and found Rev. Choi of the Pusan Central Church. "Oh, Rev. Cho, you came at just the right time. I am sure God sent you!" I didn't know what was going on. He continued, "We are in trouble with today's lecture. Originally it was planned to have Fr. Ham Se Ung and the mother of Kim Chi Ha as speakers, but they have been placed under house arrest in Seoul. Obviously this was done to block our meeting. So it has become a lecture without a lecturer. In the midst of this situation, suddenly here you are. I am sure God sent you. Please do the lecture for us."

It was no problem for me to be the speaker, but there was one special reason why I had to behave myself. I had been invited to attend the General Assembly of the World Federation of Methodist Women. I had accepted, and the person who brought the invitation told me, "You'd better be careful between now and then, or you won't get a passport from the government. You've got to participate in this assembly! So until then please act quietly." Remembering these words, I rejected the minister's request. "I am sorry, Rev. Choi. I have a particular problem that prevents me from speaking today." "You don't need to say much; just talk about the drama that was presented by the fired Dong-Il Textile Union workers at the Christian Building this past September — the liquid dung incident. Tell the story briefly; don't make it burdensome."

"Rev. Choi, please consider my situation. With my propensities, if I get up on the platform can I come down without saying what I want to say? If I once begin to speak, there's no telling what will come out of my mouth. I will do it next time — not today." Back and forth we went, and finally I was compelled to accept his insistent request. I went up on the platform and proceeded to give a fiery speech about the fight of the Dong-Il Textile workers, especially about the '78 liquid dung incident and the September prayer meeting. The audience was absorbed in my story, excited and moved. "In closing, let me say that our country is world-famous for two things: one is dictatorship, and the other is torture." The lecture meeting finished successfully.

I slept that night at the Catholic JOC. The next morning I was preparing to leave for Seoul when four strong-looking men arrived. "We are from Pusan police station. We've come to escort you to the chief of police, who wants to meet you for just ten minutes." "The chief wants to see me? There's no reason.

I don't know him and I have nothing to say to him. I must get back to Seoul quickly." "It will only take a few minutes."

We argued, and at last I went with them to Pusan police station. Contrary to their words, however, I was not taken to meet the chief, but was led directly to the information department's interrogation room. There I was questioned for seven days about the previous day's YMCA lecture. As soon as the interrogation was over, an arrest warrant was issued and I was detained in the police station jail. I felt a sense of nihility. I was not afraid of being locked in prison, but when I had not done anything special, except for speaking a few words in a lecture, the situation was absurd and exasperating.

Until I was moved to the prison, I lived in this cell and ate the terrible food provided: no rice, only barley, with a few pieces of salted radish for every meal. Thinking about this and that, at first I felt so distressed that I couldn't even sleep well. Then I thought, "This is also the will of God," and I became calm. I hoped to be moved to the prison sooner, where I looked forward to meeting the Dong-Il Textile workers for whom I had deposited the custody money a few days before. But by the time I was transferred, they had already been moved to Taegu Prison. I deeply regretted not being able to meet them.

In contrast to my first imprisonment, this time there were fewer disturbances in my day-to-day prison life. I thought, "Well, as I am here, I may as well study hard." Pusan Prison had been built fairly recently, so was very clean — quite different from the dirty and smelly Seodaemoon Prison. I even had a clean, flowered quilt, just like in a hotel. It seemed to me that the change to such a bright and clean prison atmosphere was the result of the efforts of persons such as political prisoners and prisoners of conscience who had fought for better prison conditions. I was deep in thought for some time, remembering their tears and suffering. The guard told me that the Dong-Il textile workers had been in this room before their transfer to Taegu. I felt a surge of emotion.

One day I got a written notice of arraignment. I was charged with "violation of Presidential Emergency Decree No. 9" and "violation of the Law on Meetings and Demonstrations." I read the prosecution note, which was immature and awkward. For just a few anti-government words I was being treated as if I had committed high treason. Receipt of the written arraignment meant I had to go to court for trial. I had been released from my first imprisonment without a court trial. This time was different. With many thoughts going through my mind, I could not sleep. "When I stand in court will I be able to speak well? The students who have stood trial for their student movement were very eloquent. What can I say in my summary statement?"

It was the day before the trial. At about six in the evening the woman guard opened the door and told me to come out. I was surprised, but followed her. This was unusual because as a rule the door was opened just once in the morning and once in the evening. Now it was after the evening check, and very late. I followed the guard into a room, where I saw, sitting in a chair, the prosecutor assigned to my case. He immediately got up. "Ah, Reverend. It has been a long time. You have been through much hardship." He assumed a kind expression. Then he had me sit there for four hours listening to his monologue, as he turned the topic from this to that. The main point, however, was that I should speak softly at the next day's trial, and then I would be freed. He told me my arrest had been his doing, but my release was up to me. His mission was one of appeasement.

I spent that night in agony. Should I get out, should I stay in?...Actually, without having done anything worth mentioning, it was regrettable to be imprisoned for several years. It would be more effective to get out sooner and then work harder. Tossing and turning, agonizing over what to do, I suddenly thought, "If this were Jesus, what would he do?" The answer was very clear. He would say, "Satan, go away!" Then my action, as a confessed servant of the Lord, was also very clear. I had to fight against temptation. Once I had decided, my mind became firm and at ease. If the prosecutor had not come I would not have gone through such terrible agony over my attitude at the trial. But as a result of his coming, I was ready to face my conviction.

The next morning I went to the court. The others on trial were tied with white rope. But I was handcuffed and my arms were tied at the back with several coils of green rope. There was a red sticker on my chest, as if I were a death row prisoner or spy. The other prisoners looked at me strangely. As I entered the courtroom I saw many familiar faces: ministers and priests from Pusan and workers from Inchon. At the sight of them my eyes filled with tears. I greeted them quickly with a glance. As I sat in the front row of prisoners, my heart was pounding. What if I failed? What if I stopped in the middle? To calm myself I prayed quietly to God. "Dear Lord, help me not to speak with my head but to let the Holy Spirit lead me to say what you want me to say." I felt stronger and more comfortable.

At last my turn came and the questioning started. Among other things, the prosecutor asked me, "Was not your — the defendant's — action for the purpose of class struggle?" I answered, "I do not know. I am ignorant about such things and do not understand what is meant by class struggle. I have only tried to follow the words of the Bible, acting as a shepherd to find the one lost sheep, though this means leaving the ninety-nine others to do so."

Finally the prosecutor presented his demand for sentencing. "As the prosecutor in charge of this event, I request that defendant Cho Wha Soon be penalized by seven years' imprisonment." The moment I heard this I remembered that in Rev. Park Hyung Kyu's similar case not long before, the prosecution demanded ten years of imprisonment. So I shouted loudly, "Is this sexism? You demanded ten years for Rev. Park. Why do you ask only seven years for me? Give me ten years!" The judge, prosecutor, and prison guard all looked startled.

The judge told me to make my summary statement. "I grew up in a rich home. When I was a child my home was the richest one in the village; I did not know the suffering of the poor and I never had any special difficulty in my life. When I entered prison I talked with people there and found out that most of them had experienced severe hardships in their lives, far different from me. I was surprised to hear from people my own age how hard a life they've had. When I went to the factory to work and live with the laborers, I could not help weeping in repentance. At first I met them simply to evangelize and teach the gospel, but it was no use. It was like pouring water into a bottomless jug. After a long time I realized that there is a systematic evil, and that to solve this problem it is necessary not only to worship but also to demolish that systematic evil. . . ."

I continued my story in a somewhat excited state. "In Luke's Gospel, some people came to Jesus and warned, 'Herod is trying to kill you! Please hurry and escape!' But instead of escaping, Jesus told them, 'Go and tell the fox that today and tomorrow, I will chase Satan away and heal the sick, then the third day I will finish my work. Today, tomorrow and the day after, I have to go my way. Could a prophet die anywhere else but in Jerusalem?' As a disciple of Jesus, I am doing this work with the same mind as Jesus." I turned to the courtroom audience and shouted, "Even though a crowd of devils like Herod tries to kill me, I will fight against them without fear of death. My friends the workers are the same. We will fight the devils of this land, not fearing death. The *han* [righteous anger] of all the oppressed, poor, and marginalized will turn into the sword — the dagger — of God's judgment and stab deep into the hearts of the devils. Our chief, Jesus, is leading us. We will surely have victory. Hurrah for the workers of this land! Hurrah for God!" The tears ran down my face. The judge said something to try to stop me, but none of his words were audible to me. When I finished speaking, all those in attendance stood and clapped warmly. They were all weeping.

At that moment several prison guards came running, lifted me up, and took me away. In front of the court there was a black sedan into which they threw me. As I was being driven away from the courthouse, I heard the workers calling, "Reverend, Reverend," as they tried to follow the car. One by one appeared the faces I wanted to see every day. I saw one of them fall down; she called, "Reverend..." In reaction I jumped up, but was jerked down from both sides by the guards. The workers faded from view, and my tears fell.

At the final trial I was sentenced to five years. The prosecution had demanded ten years for Rev. Hyung Kyu and he was sentenced to five years. Probably because I had demanded equal treatment as a woman, they had sentenced me to the same. I laughed quietly.

Immediately, I appealed to the higher court and was transferred to Taegu Prison. This prison was very dirty. The toilet was full of maggots, and rats came into the room through the toilet. I had a hard time with the rats. In August at my second trial I was sentenced to three years. I gave up appealing to the higher court so the sentence was confirmed. I began to serve my sentence as a convict.

On October 26, 1979, President Park Chung Hee was assassinated by one of his own men. When I heard the news I was very glad, but on the other hand I was not quite sure. I was reminded of the words of patriot Kim Ku, who fought for Korea's independence from Japan. When Korea was emancipated he said anxiously, "If it had happened just a little later, we could have accomplished our own emancipation, but it has happened by foreign power, so it has no meaning." Park's death should have been the result of the strength of our people. I was sorry it had happened the way it did.

On December 29, upon the withdrawal of Emergency Decree No. 9, most of the political prisoners were released, but I was not. Later I found out why: because I had been convicted of an additional crime, violation of the Law on Meetings and Demonstrations, and this had not been withdrawn yet. A few days later I stood in court. In the judge's room a few persons discussed the matter and then they held an informal trial. I was sentenced to one year of imprisonment and two years' suspension of execution of sentence; and a few days later I was released.

Exiting from the prison with my sack of clothing, I felt quite confused. The dictator had died.... Toward what destiny would our country now proceed? And what would by my destiny? I might have been glad because I hated Park so much, but strangely, my heart was heavy. Was it because his death was not the result of the people's power? I could not make a reasonable judgment about our political situation, but I could not rid myself of an uncomfortable premonition.

17

The Meaning of Mission

At FIRST I THOUGHT OF MISSION as making membership — bringing people into the church and making them church members. Traditionally that has been the usual method of evangelization. But when I began industrial mission work I came to know about the life of the workers. Then my established view of mission became confused. We are supposed to worship and rest on Sunday, but in the workers' case this is often impossible. For instance, at Dong-Il Textile Company, where I had my first work experience, the company schedule did not allow us to have Sunday off. It was three shifts; therefore, if I was lucky I could worship three Sundays a month; otherwise it was only twice a month.

One worker expressed her agony over her Christian life as follows. "When I lived in the countryside I attended church without missing once, but since coming to work at the factory I have been able to go to Sunday worship only once or twice a month. Even this is difficult, but I do my best. Then the pastor preached that if I do not keep Sunday holy I cannot be saved. In my situation I cannot take four Sundays a month off from work, so I became 'unable to be saved.' If I give up working this will be solved, but then how can I eat and live? It's as if I am being chased out or abandoned by the church, and my way to salvation blocked."

I was shocked personally by this worker's confession. As a pastor, I was already worried about this issue. Having heard her confession I had to think very deeply about the real meaning of mission. To comfort and encourage her, I said, "Don't worry. You didn't miss church intentionally but in order to live. You have no choice; what else can you do? God knows everything about you. You can be saved." But she went to church, taking the day off from work, and I could not judge whether she was right or wrong.

There were quite a few workers who absented themselves from work to attend church. Of course Sunday work was considered as overtime, so only that overtime pay would be subtracted from one's monthly salary. But at other companies with worse conditions, Sunday work is regarded as normal, in which case a worker who takes the day off will be penalized by the loss of three days' pay. Also, it is common for employers to work their employees harder and more severely on Sundays, sometimes demanding higher production than on weekdays. Therefore if one worker takes the day off, the others have to work more and are thrown into utter confusion. If there are ten workers, their work assignment will be for ten, so if two or three of them take the day off, the remaining seven or eight have to cover the additional work load as well as their own assignment. Thus the remaining workers come to hate and resent those who go to church, and express this in rough and abusive language. They say, "Because you go to church we have to suffer more." The group leader, cursing, will say, "What kind of guy is Jesus? Who is he? If I marry and have children I will never let them go near a church!" Hearing such words, I was shocked. Do they have to go to church on Sunday? Do we have to keep the Sabbath absolutely? I discussed these and various other issues at length with the workers, and in the process we were all gradually changed.

Probably there is no one in our society who is more trampled and pushed, this way and that, than the workers. The workers are created in God's image just the same as those who have money, power, and education, but the workers suffer under oppression. This is intolerable according to my faith. When a human being, formed in the image of God, is made to suffer unjustly and is degraded personally, isn't this the same as degrading God? Isn't the real Christian mission, then, to recover the image of these workers as they were originally created? Mission that begins and ends with the observance of Sunday worship is not real mission. The important thing is to live according to Jesus' teaching, wherever one is, struggling to restore one's rights that were taken by others, to recover one's dignity, and to defend these God-given rights — this is really the true Christian and God-fearing life.

I did not force the workers to attend church worship. I only tried to help them find themselves as they were created in God's image, and to lead them to live a Christian life according to that image. Other ministers and Christians scolded me for not being faithful, but it did not bother me because I knew I was making as great an effort as anyone to sincerely believe in and fear God and to be a true disciple of Christ. I know very well that even if there is only one person in existence who is living a subjectively perfect life, that life will have great influence on many others. By one person's life, a thousand persons' lives can be changed. One life can play the role of lever to transform social and structural evil. To do this, the individual life must be expanded toward the wider world. The monster of structural evil stands before us. It is far bigger than we, but we have to confront and fight it.

In the early stages of my UIM work I tried to concentrate on conscientization of the workers for individual change. But I came to understand that a worker conscientized in this way, however mature individually, would eventually come up against a brick wall in the process of the struggle, and there would be no way left but to compromise. At first I had not realized the great absurdity underlying the visible reality. Behind the company were always the police and the authorities, ready to intervene. The process of Dong-Il Textile Union's struggle for democratization sufficiently proved this. And how could this be only the Dong-Il case? Herein lies the reason why the labor movement cannot stop with the economic issue. I found out by experience that unless the economic struggle becomes a political issue, there can be no real meaning in the labor movement.

Since the promulgation of the Yushin Constitution in 1972, there has been a change in my direction of movement. Until then I was concerned mostly with administrative work for the labor movement, but from 1972 I became involved in political action, stirring up political awareness, and struggling for political change. Naturally, the workers who were closely related to me were influenced and began to develop political inclinations. They came to recognize the structural enemy, and they studied social science until they understood it better than I. It was a great development. Their main fighting slogans were no longer "Increase wages" and "Improve working conditions," but rather "Let us live as humans" and "Do not oppress democratic labor union activities." This was a gesture of human liberation. The words themselves did not have a political character, but the emphasis on the right of unity and the right of union activity was more political than economic.

The government would not stand for this. Even the democratization of the company labor unions was already a threat. Now, as the labor union workers were developing political consciousness, the government saw itself facing a serious crisis. Nothing causes more apprehension in a capitalist society than the laborers. If the government could not grasp the reins of the labor union, there was no telling what might happen, or when. Furthermore, any government such as ours that maintained its political power by means of oppressing the laborers could not think of loosening its grip on the labor unions. This is why attempts to destroy the labor unions — such as the dung-throwing incident — were inevitable. The government leaders could get a good night's sleep only when they had crushed at its roots all autonomous grassroots organization.

But the laborers do not fall easily. For the mere reason that they took part in the labor movement, many workers have been fired, have had their names put on a "blacklist," and even suffered imprisonment. But this suffering has rather made them braver and stronger. They are still fighting in the ranks of the labor movement, withstanding many difficulties. I am convinced that this kind of labor movement is true mission. Jesus came to this world in the form of a human being to proclaim liberation and freedom to the poor and oppressed. Who are the oppressed in this land today? Where is Jesus present? What is the life of a true disciple of Jesus? I found the answers to all these questions in my life together with the laborers, and in my commitment to the labor movement.

18

Laborers' Consciousness

LIFE ITSELF MAKES MOVEMENT. The theory, strategy, and tactics of movement are not something you can learn from books. The labor movement is created by one's awakening in the midst of the reality of the laborers' life. Previously knowing nothing about UIM, this is the kind of awakening that I experienced as I lived with the workers during the past eighteen years. This applies not only to me, but is clearly seen in the life and movement of the workers near me. Among my friends who are women workers, one of the closest is Kim Yong Ja. She was a leader of the campaign to abolish the "blacklist," which was a main issue in the 1984 Korean labor movement; originally, she was one of the 126 women who were fired in the 1978 Dong-Il Textile Union struggle.

Anyone who sees only the famous fighter, the passionate and intense Kim Yong Ja of today, could probably not imagine her earlier image. At the time when she had just joined the labor movement, she was very quiet, she seemed to feel inferior, and at every meeting she shrank into the corner. She did not know how to express herself clearly and she could not be at ease with the other workers who explained the labor movement theoretically. What enabled her to emerge as an active, self-confident movement leader in front of her other friends who were fired? Actually, at the time there were many other very intelligent and capable laborers.

Kim Yong Ja's living conditions were different from the others. Her home was in the country; she had no relatives and no place to stay in Inchon, while her friends had homes and parents there. Those workers who were from the country eventually went back home and married. But Yong Ja did not go back. There was just one reason: It was not because of the movement but only because of her simple compassion, or maybe I can call it loyalty. She could not leave her friends and her minister who were fighting for reinstatement and go back to the comforts of home alone. She did not have confidence in the movement but stayed in Inchon only because of her good heart.

For a worker labeled by the blacklist, life in a strange city without any help is like hanging on the edge of a cliff. She imagines how heavenly it would be not to have been dismissed and to still be working at the factory. A fired worker has no place to go. Having left the dormitory, it is hard to find even a place to sleep, let alone sufficient food. She wanders around in the streets, spending one day with one friend, the next with another. When she runs out of money, she has to borrow from her friends. Due to this irregular and unsettled life, she develops illness.... Then she makes up her mind to go back to work; if only the company does not fire her she will work hard. Survival comes first; only when one's existence is certain is a labor movement possible.

But even with her mind thus set, the reality does not allow her to keep silent. "I won't get involved this time. I have to earn money for the rent." But seeing the young workers, suffering under the company's deception and vicious low wages, she becomes angry enough to catch fire, and she ends up getting involved in another fight. For this she is fired again. The more often she is fired the tougher her living becomes. But the only place she finds to sleep is the factory; therefore she continues to be in the center of reality where the movement is, and there she experiences her own being and the development of the movement. This was the situation of Kim Yong Ja.

In the case of workers who have a place to stay nearby, even if they are fired they don't suffer the tension of basic survival, and thus they tend to leave the company if even small difficulties arise. Staying around the fringes of the movement for a long time turns one's movement theory into a dead theory. Such a theory is a repeating of the past. It has lost its vitality to fight and overcome the enemy. All movement theory becomes mature through fierce fighting from the center of life.

Ψ

Let me tell the story of the strike led by Kim Yong Ja — a fine and impressive one, which took place when she was a bus girl in 1982.* Yong Ja could no longer get a factory job anywhere, so she went to work as a bus girl in the early part of 1982, at an Inchon city bus company. She made up her mind to stay there until she had saved one million won, the amount needed to rent a room by the Kye money system. (The renter deposits a large sum of money, which is returned at the end of the term of residence; the rent is paid by the interest from the deposit.) She was ready to endure any difficulty. But the working conditions and pay level were poor beyond an ordinary person's imagination. Furthermore, her fellow workers had become extremely dehumanized by their situation.

One day Yong Ja came to see me; she was cursing her fellow workers. "They are not the least bit like human beings. You know I have been here only a few weeks, but all my blouses have been stolen. Every time I get up in the morning I find another thing missing. The room looks terrible. They have all grown up with savage manners and it is like hell on earth. You know what happened, Reverend? One girl was very sick; she could not sleep and was groaning. Then the girl who had been sleeping beside her swore at her, 'Shut up! Why are you making that groaning sound? Because of you I cannot sleep!' What kind of person is that? I have been around many places, but I've never seen this kind of thing before."

Although I did not know the details of the situation, I was not quite happy about her cursing her fellow workers like that, and felt distressed. Then, three months later, Yong Ja came again and told me, "Reverend, remember last time when I was so critical of the other girls and was cursing them? I was wrong. It is not they who are bad. Since I've been living and working with them, I can understand everything. They are too, too miserable. I am also getting dehumanized. In this work there is no way but to get like that. Since the curfew was lifted we are the ones left with the deadly hard work. The time we get up in the morning is the same, but the evening working time has been extended. On top of this, if there is a shortage of girls or if someone is out sick, the regular alternate-day shift schedule is abandoned and we have to work two or three days in succes-

---

*It was the job of bus girls, or conductors, to stand at the rear door of the bus, get the passengers on and off quickly, collect the fares, and assist the driver.

sion, or sometimes even for a whole week. During this time, no matter how exhausted we are, we can get no more than one or two hours of sleep a night. Do you know how hard the work is? At morning and evening rush hours we have to take cursing from the passengers and irritating treatment from the driver, whatever the condition of our health. And with the rat's tail salary we get, isn't it natural for the bus girls to pocket some of the money from the fares? And doesn't the company strip-search us because of the fare-pocketing problem? We cannot even think of ourselves as human beings. When we get overly tired and irritable our nerves are sometimes so on edge that we would like to give up everything in the world, and even feel like grabbing and eating up the nearest person. Under the circumstances, how can they be concerned about their sick neighbors? The situation forces them to steal, to hate each other, and to fall into continual arguments with one another."

Kim had come to feel deep compassion and affection for her fellow workers. At the same time she realized that the situation must be reformed, and that struggle was the only path to reform. She began to work on two things. One was to create an atmosphere in which her fellow workers could look at themselves and feel a renewed compassion toward their friends. The other was to rally the core members to strike. The notoriously clean and tidy Yong Ja decided first of all to clean up the room where she was living, and to wash all the socks, underwear, and handkerchiefs lying around. That was not easy work, because there was an inadequate supply of running water. There were only four water taps serving the more than ninety workers in the dormitory, so at morning and night it was a scene of utter confusion. Everybody wanted to wash quickly, but while they argued with each other, the water and the time ran away. After all the other workers had finished washing, Yong Ja did her roommates' laundry. Her sleeping hours got that much shorter, but it was joyful work of overflowing love. She folded the clean and dry clothes and put them where everybody could find them. She cleaned the room by herself. At first nobody paid any attention, but after a few days they began to notice. "Wow, who is doing this every day? Who is it?" Gradually they began to express concern for one another.

There were few toilets in the dormitory. The workers always

complained, "They're dirty," but never cleaned them. Then Yong Ja began cleaning them alone. The other girls naturally began to follow the good and diligent Yong Ja; they listened to what she said, and trusted her. In spite of many difficulties, the dormitory atmosphere improved.

Meantime, Yong Ja began to meet with a small group of trustworthy and courageous workers. They formed a "kye," something like a credit union, and at their meetings they talked about working conditions, wages, etc., focusing on what they could do about the inhuman treatment of the bus conductors. They finally decided to have a strike, with Yong Ja as the leader. Even though she was known all over Inchon, there was no one else with the necessary experience. So she prepared herself to go to prison. With her long experience Yong Ja planned the strike in careful detail. For security, she did not tell even her close partners any unnecessary information. I did not know about the plans at all. Just a few hours before the designated day I got a phone call. Yong Ja's urgent voice said, "Reverend, I need some money. Could you lend me some?" Then I knew something was going on.

The event started at two o'clock in the morning when everybody was sleeping. Yong Ja got up alone. Since work began at 4 a.m., she had to finish everything secretly before that time. The place of the strike was not at the company, which would have been difficult; she had reserved a room at an inn in the next village. The plan was to move the whole group to that place for the sit-in strike. However the company might try to pacify them, not a single worker should betray the strike, because that would damage both the process and the results of the struggle. Everybody had gotten the message except for a few pro-company workers and section chiefs, so they expected no problem. But in order to be certain, Yong Ja threw all the work clothes into a big drum of water. Now, even if the company persuasion was strong, or some workers lacked courage, there were no work clothes to wear; so how could one work? Yong Ja anticipated the situation correctly.

The next thing was to cut a hole in the fence around the dormitory, for an escape exit. The working conditions were so bad that sometimes the workers wanted to resign, but the company did not permit them to do so. Those who wanted to resign had

to run away. In order to prevent such escapes, the company
had erected a steel-wire fence around the compound. Yong Ja
started to cut the steel wire with a tool she had obtained. It
was really very hard work with her thin, weak hands. She was
soon sweating all over and her hands were bleeding. Her heart
was pounding hard. But she had to cut the hole. For the first
time, she prayed urgently with all her heart. "God, ninety lives
are depending on this. If this wire does not get cut we will die.
Please, let it be cut!" She felt new strength, and the wire started
to give way. After one hour of hard effort, making as little noise
as possible, she had made a hole large enough for one person to
get through.

She then went to the dormitory and woke the others. One by
one they stealthily crept out through the fence, until the last one
had escaped. Yong Ja led them to the waiting truck that was to
take them to the next village. It was a big exodus in the silent
darkness. Suddenly they heard dogs barking. They all held their
breath. A night guard appeared, blowing his whistle. "What in
the world are you young ladies doing out so early in the morning." "We're going to early morning prayer meeting," Yong Ja
replied promptly, but sweating hard. The guard looked around
at them, then went on his way. There were no further problems
on the way to the inn. All the preparations had finished before
four o'clock.

Meanwhile, at the company, great confusion had arisen. As
usual, at 3:30, the loudspeaker sounded to wake the workers
in advance of their 4:00 starting time. Nobody showed up.
The confused company people turned on the emergency alarm,
opened the doors, and ran into the workers' rooms. They found
nobody there. Shouting loudly for them, they ran all over the
village, to the hill behind, and the public bath. Unable to run the
buses at rush hour, they got complaints from the citizens, and
the Inchon city traffic was confused. The company did not know
what to do about this sudden happening. The workers' where-
abouts were made known at 10 a.m., when a worker phoned
to present a six-point request for a wage raise, improvement of
working conditions, and a better working atmosphere. Upon
the company's receipt of this message, fifteen agents were immediately dispatched to the striking place. Plainclothes police
and riot troops densely surrounded the inn and commanded the

workers to disperse. Inside the room where the strike was going on, the workers expressed fear of the powerful response by the company and police. The experienced Yong Ja calmed them down: "If we are united, we will have victory." The strikers locked the doors from inside to prevent any forced dispersal. Then they wrote their six articles on papers and hung them on the wall. They shouted in unison, "Thirty percent wage raise; install fans in the dormitory; improve the water system," etc., and sang songs.

In the closed, small room, full of the smell of people and sweat, it was hard to breathe, but they embraced each other and continued their desperate resistance. Even the police, who could hear their demands, felt sympathetic. Their working conditions were so bad, and their requests were the very minimum. Then a message came from the company suggesting negotiations. The company said they would listen to all the requests. Yong Ja, having experienced company deceit many times through verbal "promises," asked that the president come and sign a written promise in front of the workers.

Meanwhile, the police began to come up a ladder into the room. The forcible dispersion started. As the door was opened and fresh air came in, the first began to pass out, one by one — a combined result of shock and the release of tension. The police shouted, "You bitches, what kind of drug did you take, and what kind of show is this?" They threw the girls outside as if they were luggage. But by that time all the requests had been accepted.

The bus girls returned to work as usual. The strike had gone on for six hours. That evening the police tried to find the leader, who until then had been unknown. Yong Ja and five other girls were taken away. When news of this arrest spread to those who were working in the buses, they all stopped working and came together to re-enter the strike. The police promised to release the six promptly, saying the detention was just a formality. But during the investigation they found out that Yong Ja had been fired from Dong-Il Textile Company, and this threw them into a state of confusion. They changed the direction of the investigation completely, focusing on the connections with the fired Dong-Il Textile workers, Kim Yong Ja, UIM, and Cho Wha Soon. The promised release time was nearing, and the workers' demands for release were getting stronger. The police finally freed all the workers.

As Yong Ja was released the workers embraced each other and "made a joyful noise." By the next day the company atmosphere had changed to nearly resemble heaven. For breakfast there was meat soup, and the broadcast announcements were gentle and polite. The workers were so moved by the changed atmosphere that their eyes became hot with tears. "Cry, then you'll get milk. Cry!"

The next day there were signs that Yong Ja might be detained again. She escaped, and was running for some time. While she was in hiding her living was more difficult, but her fellow workers who had been with her in the strike secretly raised funds for her and helped her get along.

Ψ

In countries with a political and economic structure similar to Korea's, it is characteristic that students and intellectuals play an important role in the resistance movement. This was true of the labor movement in Korea in the 1970s. The suicide by self-immolation of Peace Market worker Chun Tae Il in November 1970 was the spark that turned the labor movement into a social issue. From that time the labor issue has been recognized as an important task for the student, intellectual, and religious movements, and the trend has been to seek the motivating power for social development in the labor movement. Accordingly, many intellectuals were concerned about the labor movement and tried to develop it through meeting with the laborers in various ways. But there were many difficulties, due to the basically different lifestyles and social positions of those who were meeting together to try to develop as equal partners.

The most serious problem revealed in these meetings was the gap between the laborers and the intellectuals. It would be appropriate to evaluate the level of development of the labor movement over the past ten years by focusing on and assessing the process by which this contradiction was overcome. Even now, the great task of our movement, as laborers or intellectuals, is to contribute to the whole movement, while fully preserving our ongoing branch movements.

Looking at the labor movement from this perspective and on the basis of my eighteen-year-long industrial mission experience, I think there are three steps in the development of workers' awareness. We can say that the process of this development moves toward the workers' building an autonomous and independent self-movement structure and then toward their building solidarity in equality with other movements. In the first step, if I explain it graphically, the intellectual is on an upper level and the laborer on a lower level in the relationship. This is the phenomenon when the laborer does not yet have a *"minjung"* (people) consciousness and the intellectual with the will for movement enters the situation. The intellectuals believe that they have to help the people, who are not yet conscious of their own historical subjectivity, to become conscious so that they can fight against the oppressive structure.

On the other side, the laborer feels a sense of inferiority as well as respect for the intellectual, who opens up a new world to one who is living in an illiterate and closed world. The laborer experiences the beginning of historical awareness and begins to struggle. At this stage the role of the intellectual is great. The laborers feel unconditional gratitude, respect, and trust toward these benefactors who have opened up a new future to them. The intellectuals feel a corresponding responsibility to awaken the laborers.

But soon this turns upside down. The laborers, who have — through their own bodily experience — begun to recognize themselves as historical subjects, begin to reject the intellectuals. This is because the more the relationship develops, the deeper the awareness becomes of the gap between their different life situations. The laborers declare, "We will solve everything by ourselves." They enter a phase in which they unconditionally reject everything connected with the intellectuals and deal with all matters uncompromisingly, exclusively, and self-righteously. In this process, the rejected intellectuals feel anger toward the laborers who are no longer "obedient" and may separate from them; otherwise they go through the necessary birth pangs to transcend this process. This is the second step.

The third step is maturity. The laborers come to realize that a movement premised on unconditional rejection of the intellectuals will inevitably be a crippled movement. They come to understand that a competitive mindset, excessive consciousness of themselves as victims, and exclusiveness have a bad effect on the whole situation and evaluation of their capability, and will finally bring mistaken practice and results. Then they understand that they should be broadened for a greater purpose, and they begin to cooperate in a relationship of equality to discover what kind of cart they are pushing for the development of history, and what to do to keep the wheels of that cart rolling smoothly. This is the level of understanding we must reach not only in the labor movement but in the whole society.

My basic principle for laborers' conscientization is very simple. It is that "the laborers are also persons created in the image of God. They are no different from the minister, the company president, or the president of the country; they are not inferior to these others. Each laborer, though seemingly nothing special, has the image of God inside; the only problem is that she is not aware of this." Accordingly, it is my task to help her discover the image of God inside herself. Once a laborer finds self-confidence, then she becomes free of dependence on others and able to do everything well. This point is very important. But around us we can see many ministers and intellectuals whose understanding and actions are contrary to this. They are caught up by the idea that they are teaching the laborers, perhaps "bestowing" something on them. This is a tragedy. With this attitude all will be finished at the second step mentioned above. There will be division and the movement will be stopped. The general level of our UIM work also seems to be remaining at this second stage. For either intellectuals or laborers to develop to the third step, they must go through the suffering of birth pangs, that is, must give themselves up and see the greater whole. If we insist on our own side as the center and maintain an exclusiveness, without seeing the whole situation and our partner's equal role, then what is the ultimate difference between us and the "dictator" whom we criticize and struggle against?

19

"The Kim Dae Jung
Rebellion Plot"

How will historians of the future evaluate the spring of 1980 in Korea? President Park had been assassinated by his own man, Kim Jae Kyu, the former head of the KCIA, and Kim Jae Kyu had then been executed. As soon as Park died, the government proclaimed martial law, and everywhere we went we saw armed soldiers, solemnly guarding. All the universities were closed. Students and citizens, wherever they went, found themselves gathering in impromptu groups of two or three, five or six, to try to predict the outcome of this emergency political situation and sense the prospects for the democratization struggle. Many intellectuals, laborers, and students, using this golden opportunity that had brought the collapse of the dictator's group, worked hard to achieve a new, democratic society.

Meanwhile, however, very careful preparations were under way for the entry of a new military government. As I watched the spring of 1980, I had the ominous feeling that this was like a second May 16th (the coup d'etat of Park Chung Hee). I was not wrong. From midnight on May 17, the emergency martial law was expanded and warrants for the arrest of Kim Dae Jung and many other democratic figures were dispatched. Reactionary suppression was begun against the fierce democratization struggle, which had been continuing, and it was immediately clear that power had been seized by a strong new group.

That morning, around two o'clock, I was taken from my home by KCIA agents to the Seoul Namsan KCIA center. I had been there several times so I knew the place very well, but this time I was taken to a deeper place underground, at the second basement level. First they changed my clothes for an army uniform. This was my first such experience; it may have been to instill fear of the martial law, and it had the effect. Then they took me into a small room less than six feet square. Four male interrogators sat facing me on the other side of a table. They proceeded to create a terrifying atmosphere, speaking to me in cold, hard, snake-like voices. "See here, now things are different. You may have been treated well before, as a minister, but not any more. Attention!" Peremptorily, they talked down to me, using low form.* "What on earth is this? I don't know why I have been brought here." "Shut up! Don't say anything!" Actually, since my release in 1979 I had not been involved in any political issue directly; therefore my question was reasonable.

The door was open, and several interrogators I had seen before looked in, remarking cynically, "Oh, here you are again! You come often!" The interrogators in front of me, looking at this scene, exclaimed, "What in blazes! How big a figure this woman must be; she knows a higher ranking interrogator that I don't even know. But it's no use!" I had been interrogated many times before, but this time was absolutely different. It was fear itself. I felt my body shrinking and losing strength.

They first focused briefly on my connections with the Dong-Il Textile workers who had been carrying on a hunger strike at the Federation of Korean Trade Unions office in Yoido until the day before, demanding reinstatement. Then, putting that aside as if it were nothing, they plunged into a concentrated inquiry into my connections with Kim Dae Jung. The scenario of those supposed connections was already set up. They said that I had met him and received money from him; that I gave the money to the late Chun Tae Il's sister Chun Soon Ok, to stir up the laborers; and further, that I had agitated the students to plot rebellion. What they demanded was for me to confess this.

I felt like I was suffocating. None of it was true. Indeed it was nothing but their manufactured scenario. I sensed that a great plot was being carried out. The method of interrogation was not questioning on the various contents of their accusations, but demanding that I confirm their already set-up scenario. Naturally, the atmosphere was one of terror.

I denied the scenario. I claimed I had never met Kim Dae Jung. Actually, I had met him once when he came to Inchon

---

*The Korean language has various honorific and non-honorific forms that are used according to the positions of those addressed. The use of low form (except among intimate friends) is an insult.

Dapdong Cathedral for a speech, but political issues were not mentioned, and furthermore I had never received any money or plotted anything. Therefore I absolutely denied all that they said.

After I was interrogated for two days in the basement, I was taken to the second floor. It was a pleasant place with a double bed, sofa, refrigerator, toilet, and even a bathtub. The interrogators said Kim Dae Jung's room and mine were the best ones. I discovered that Rev. Moon Ik Whan was two rooms away from me; I could hear his unmistakable voice. I found out that Kim Dae Jung and Lee Hae Dong were in the same building.

The interrogation continued. I heard continual sounds of beatings and screams from the next room. The interrogators threatened me, saying they would strip me naked and torture me. Even if I was accustomed to being interrogated, this atmosphere terrified me. I was so afraid that once I even begged for my life without realizing what I was doing.

I was feeling like I might have a heart attack, and I also felt that if I stayed there any longer I would become mentally disturbed. I had heard that many interrogators suffer from heart disease, because they live in a closed space, day in and day out. Around me there was no trace of nature except the air. The building was completely closed to the outside; there was no glimpse of the outside. I begged the interrogators to let me see the sky for just a moment. More than anything else, I wanted to see the sky. One evening, as though he'd remembered what I'd said, one high-ranking interrogator came in (apparently slightly drunk) and said, "Hey, Reverend, I will do something for you. Follow me and I will let you see the sky, but don't try to see both sides." Then he took me out. The other interrogator tried to stop him because if those above him found this out, something terrible would happen. But he did not listen to them and resolutely led me out. He opened the steel door and I could see the sky for just a few seconds. It was the night sky and it was beautiful. I felt an immensely cool sensation as if my heart had been drilled open. Once again I felt how precious and beautiful was the nature created by God.

Another time the electricity was out, and in that basement when the lights were out it was darkness itself. I could feel the dark as something tangible, and was afraid. I realized how precious a thing is light. If we did not have light, how dreadful this world would be.

They abused me with sexual innuendos, all sorts of cursing and psychological pressure to try to get me to sign their manufactured scenario. I was exhausted. They did not beat me because I was a woman, but it was hard to bear the pressure. The others had physical torture as well, so their suffering must have been unspeakable. In spite of all my suffering I denied the scenario. As the first four interrogators had failed to make me submit, a veteran interrogator took over and began to re-interrogate me. He prevented me from sleeping and used streams of terrible curses to shrink my spirit. I was so tired I did not care about anything. I only wished this nightmare would come to an end somehow.

Looking at myself, I suddenly felt like a miserable, servile insect. At that moment I thought I would rather die than live in this servile form. "Yes, it would be better to die. Whether I die this way or another way, it's still death. When have I been afraid of death?" Then, not knowing from where I had gotten such courage, I glared at the interrogator and shouted, "You low-bred dog! Kill me if you want to! I told you, a minister does not lie. Even if you cut my throat, what is not, is not. I don't want to live any longer, so kill me, I said, you lower-than-dogs!" The interrogator suddenly held up his hands in surrender. "I've failed!" he said, and went out. I was also surprised.

After that, they did not insist on making me agree. Instead they requested me to make a statement on "What I think about Kim Dae Jung." I said to myself, "Ah, it's almost finished!" Probably their practice was to tighten up if one became more submissive, and loosen up if one stood up strongly against the pressure. Is this perhaps the nature of so-called bureaucracy? They were ready to tape my statement. This was customarily taken in writing, but now they taped my voice directly. I answered, turning my story around. "I respect Kim Dae Jung. I've always thought he committed himself, risking his neck for our nation and people. Then I heard here that he was a spy and plotted the national upheaval. It is different from what I have known of him before, but if it is true I will never meet him again." The interrogator took the tape and after a while he came back. "It was rejected, you have to speak more moderately." Then he taped it again and it was passed, he said.

On July 20, 1980, I was released. Those seventy days of interrogation were like a nightmare. Instead of joy over my release, however, I felt sorry toward the others for my coming out alone. On the way out I asked to meet Rev. Moon Ik Whan, but they refused. Throwing off their hands, I ran into Rev. Moon's room. He was pacing back and forth, with his hands clasped behind his back. "Reverend, I'm sorry, I'm going out before you." I was about to cry. Rev. Moon said nothing, but embraced and kissed me. My steps on the way home were heavy, as if my feet weighed a thousand pounds. My mind would have been more at ease if I'd been put in prison.

Later, the so-called Kim Dae Jung Rebellion Plot was in the papers, and the part connected with me was printed just the same as the first KCIA scenario, even though I had denied it. In the future this remnant of false history will be judged as such.

20

Back to the Factory

BEING DEEPLY CONNECTED to the labor movement in the 1970s through industrial mission, I became aware of the absolute necessity of expanding the movement among the grassroots people. A people's movement, no matter how urgently needed, cannot be actualized through the unity of a few intellectuals. In a people's movement, the people must be the subject. Only when the people move can a new society be made. No matter how nicely the political situation is changed, if organization and power are not secured among the grassroots people, nothing will have been achieved. Of course, there will be some development of the process.

Looking back later at the political whirlpools of 1979 and the 1980s and the shape of our movement's response, I could understand the situation more clearly. I had a touch of fantasy then that everything would be better since Park Chung Hee had died. Park's regime had been so extremely repressive that it had placed deadly limits on all the fields of movement. During the previous ten years I had given many public political speeches, which was the reason I was detained several times and was on the surveillance list. I had been living in Inchon but going back and forth to Seoul just like it was my home, as I became fervently involved in lecture meetings, prayer meetings, and counter-measures committees for big incidents, etc.

But this kind of movement lacked the power to reform our society in 1979 and 1980. The decisive element was the power of the grassroots people. When there is tight organization and fighting power starting from the grassroots, the political struggle, like a living spark, will blaze into a great power for change. What I understood then, looking at the situation of our country's movement power, was that it was necessary to have organized movement rooted deep in the grassroots rather than in the political intellectual movement, and I decided to take up the task of implementing that understanding. The gathering of a few intellectuals or ministers to make new organizations and carry out activities according to their particular views is problematic for a real movement. Real power comes from common practice connected with the grassroots people.

Having reached this understanding, I no longer came to Seoul so frequently. I thought it was more important to spend my life meeting more laborers, however I could do this. I went into semi-hiding, and because I was being watched by the KCIA in Inchon, I had my residence recorded as my sister's home. I rented a room elsewhere and spent my time with the laborers. It was a period (1981) when many laborers were disappointed and discouraged because the democratic labor unions and movement power they had fought so hard to achieve in the 1970s were now in the process of being harshly trampled and broken. I told them, "Let's live again, work hard and build the movement again. Be strong!" Comforting and encouraging them, I gathered the scattered workers together again.

But this kind of activity was limited to contacts with those I had known before. Though it was important to discuss and plan things with them, their activities were under some limitations, so there was a problem in solving the task of expansion of the base of grassroots workers. While I was thinking about what to do, I decided to enter a factory to get back into the workers' reality. My goal was to work with laborers in the factory, meet grassroots workers, and help them organize themselves. I was fifty years old, but I used my thirty-seven-year-old sister-in-law's residence card to get hired — partly because of my age but also because I did not want my former record to be known. I had my hair cut to make myself look younger, and dyed it to hide the white in it.

The factory where I went to work made cotton underwear. It was not such hard work, but one new development was that people treated me as an *ajumma* (aunt). I had not expected this and was rather unpleasantly surprised. While I was working with young people I had not thought about my age. In fact, I lived as a young person. But here I was nothing but an *ajumma*. An *ajumma* who went out to work was simultaneously the object of sympathy and contempt because people thought, "Poor thing, to have to go to work at her age!"

In any event, I had no technical skills, so I had to do the most undesirable work. Even eighteen- and nineteen-year-old women made me do errands for them, and the language they used was very low. Of course, in the factory the technician was king. It must have been natural to look down on me for lack of technical expertise, and especially the young technicians seemed to think of me as an unfortunate *ajumma* — they never treated me as a laborer.

As I worked and lived with these laborers, I repented deeply once again. I understood anew how precious the laborer's life is — how valuable the reality of their life is. I was deeply moved, feeling in touch with the true meaning of life, something I could not achieve through my sermons in church. This precious awareness arose in the process of my breaking and giving myself up. Regardless, I was sometimes so angry over my bad treatment by young laborers that I shouted silently, "You brats, who do you think I am, to laugh at me? I am the very Cho Wha Soon!" Outside I was well-known and respected but in the factory I was an object of scorn, which was psychologically hard to endure. It was childish and shameful of me, but I had a hidden desire to show them I was the famous movement leader Cho Wha Soon.

One day I made a mistake because of this attitude. I told some young laborers, "I would like to invite you to my home. Will you come?" I used the word *cho-dae* (invite), a rather formal term of Chinese origin. Usually my language was very easy and informal. The words I used were fitted to everyday living and I generally avoided using Chinese or English. In 1974 when I was arrested, in fact, I was misunderstood because of my use of simple language: the investigators accused me of using such language intentionally to get close to people so I could stir them up. Actually I never tried to use easy language for agitative purposes, but just came to it naturally by living with the laborers for a long time. I could not remember having used the term *cho-dae* for a long time: I hadn't been in such a high cultural milieu. Then how did this forgotten word suddenly pop out?

When I'd said "I would like to invite you," the laborers' eyes widened in surprise. Invite? *Cho-dae?* They were probably reminded of the scene of a luxurious party they had seen on TV. "Inviting" is for such people and in such a place, not for laborers working in a factory fourteen hours a day, because it had nothing to do with their culture. Their curious expressions shocked me into awareness. "Oh, I've made a mistake!" I thought. This unfortunate nobody, this *ajumma* used a high-level intellectual word! My inner desire to show off was manifested like that.

I thought about Jesus Christ. Jesus came to serve human beings in a human shape. He came from the highest place to the lowest place. Being nowhere as high as Jesus, still I hesitated to be lower. Even when I thought I was going to have to move one step down, it gave me so much pain!

When students concerned about the labor movement would go to work in the factory, they would come to me to ask how to proceed, and I always told them, "Leadership of the labor movement does not come through dominating them and teaching them. That is not real leadership. The true way is to learn through the laborers and make the movement with them. We must get rid of such titles as 'intellectual' and 'minister.' I do not know how far this is possible, but we must practice to give ourselves up, to be lower. It is really self-training to overcome our weak point as intellectuals — the tendency to fall into the dogmatism of one's own theory."

And now, when I was in the factory with the workers, I had made the same mistake. I had been proud. Wasn't that why I had used the word *cho-dae?* At first the laborers were surprised, but immediately their reaction changed: "Invite us? Really? How nice, we are invited!"

The next day they came to my house and we ate dinner together, sharing conversation. Of course it was not as fine a party as they might have imagined, but for those who were worn out by living it was a time of excitement and relaxation. After that, the laborers seemed to think, "This *ajumma* is not the kind to work at a place like this. She is different from other *ajummas*." If they thought like that and observed me, they would find that I really was different from the others, because I was not a laborer. From then, if they had something they did not know, they came to me and asked about it. Sometimes they wanted counselling about boys, and sometimes translation of English terms on product labels. I had become familiar with them, but I was already judged as an outsider.

I reflected on many things through this experience. I found

out that during the past years, though I had thought I was with the laborers, laughing and crying with them and living an active life with them, it was not as I'd thought, nor was my movement activity what I had thought. I was ashamed of myself. It seemed that I had nothing to say about the movement. As the same kind of laborer, this *ajumma* should have been accepted as a poor person, and from her real situation should come her life story, leading to the common question, "What shall we do?" But if they treated me like this I became a different *ajumma* — an educated and intellectual *ajumma*.

There was an additional problem. I was wondering how to answer if people asked what my husband did. I was going to say he had gone to Saudi Arabia (as a temporary laborer). But when I discussed this with a few friends, they said it would not work. That was because among married women laborers there were many wives whose husbands had gone to Saudi Arabia, and they would ask, "Where in Saudi Arabia?" which company, how much was his pay, what kind of work did he do, etc. Then it would be very difficult to answer. So I told them he had gone to the United States. But that was a mistake. For them there was a big difference between going to the Middle East and going to the U.S.A. They shared the common belief that anyone who is able to go to the U.S. is rich, while a person who goes to Saudi Arabia is poor. In this case no matter how well I explained it, it was no use. Therefore, my having a husband in the U.S. to earn money made me different from other *ajummas*.

I had a similar problem with my clothing. I tried to be humble and look shabby, wearing blue jeans and a T-shirt, but it was strange to the laborer's eyes. It was then popular to wear suits and nice-looking blouses and try to look attractive. Though I'd thought my style would appeal to them, on the contrary it looked shabby and different. Actually, at that age, who would wear blue jeans?

I finally had to quit working after three months. There was another reason why this came to pass. As I mentioned before, I had used my sister-in-law's residence card for my job application, and one day I had to fill out a form on my family situation for medical insurance. My sister-in-law had three children, the youngest a three-year-old. At my age, having a three-year-old child did not look right, so I was not quite sure what to do, but since it was on the record I had to write it like that. It bothered me, though.

About a week later, the group chief came to me and said, "*Ajumma,* you don't look like you have a three-year-old child. Did you perhaps use someone else's residence card?" I could not say anything, I was so anxious not to have my situation uncovered. "Tell me the truth. Now I am the only one who knows this, but don't you see there will be trouble if our department chief finds out? You do not look so poor — why are you working at a place like this? Why don't you quit before anybody finds out who you are?" I was sure he did not know who I was, but since I was already worried about the possible problems, I decided to quit. As payday was just a few days away, I said I would quit right after that. So I came to work the next day; but I could not work well, I was so uncomfortable. If my name were disclosed then it would be terrible. It wouldn't be only my problem, but would cause much trouble for other movement workers. If the government found out people my age were working in the factory using fake names, it was very clear that they would investigate all the factories and labor field to weed out all the young movement workers. At that time, in fact, there were many students working in factories.

When I had first decided to go back to the factory, the young people heard about it and came running to try to dissuade me. "What is this? Reverend, are you out of your mind? Unfortunately, you know that if you get caught, it won't be only you who is finished. It will affect all the others who don't even have any relation to you. Please don't go into the factory." Remembering these words I could not stand it any longer. If I waited till payday and something happened, what could I do? I quit the next day. As it turned out, this was a fortunate decision, because the management of the company was transferred to the welfare department of the government and it became a government factory. All the papers were carefully inspected. It was good that I quit before any problems arose.

Ψ

After I finished my direct involvement in the labor reality, I thought and reflected for a long time. I terribly regretted my inadequacy. I had always been thinking I had to do movement work not only through words but through my living, and yet I still had the superior attitude of an intellectual and the pride of a movement worker.

I began to agonize over another problem. If I wanted to work for expansion of a people's grassroots movement, what kind of attitude and approach did I need? With this concern I watched movement people and found many things not quite satisfactory to me. Quite a few women workers in the movement drank and smoked and I had many talks with them about this. To expand the grassroots movement among women workers, the method should be the people's way. To the newcomer, how would it look to have women smoking? Up to now, smoking and drinking have not been open to women in Korean society. If one sees a woman smoking or drinking, one does not feel favorably toward her. To a plain and simple worker she is the image of the corrupt: a hostess at a restaurant, a waitress, or a prostitute. She will get a rejecting response. If someone talks about grassroots expansion while smoking or drinking, she will get no trust from the ordinary laborers, nor any respect. Most people feel comfortable going along with the common sense and customs of the society, and reasonable explanations to the contrary will not work in many cases. If grassroots people feel uncomfortable with the behavior of a person, they will not accept her, however beautiful her movement goals may sound.

To approach the people one should adopt a more popular and flexible method, which means giving up exceptional living styles. One's lifestyle must enable one to breathe together with the people. This does not mean following the popular masses, but rather starting from there, in such a way that one can be a leader respected and loved by the people. Actually, an extraordinary lifestyle will segregate one from the people due to one's self-important attitude or pride.

If we really think seriously about the movement and want to change ourselves for it, we must go through the pain of breaking. The task for the movement of the 1980s is for all its sectors to expand and take root from the bottom, gathering the grassroots people's power. The student movement, the Christian movement, whatever the movement, it must create its share. In fact all the movement forces seem to share this same idea.

Contrary to this conclusion, some participating intellectuals — of course, not all — have an attitude that says, "You follow me, whatever we do. That is the only way." The laborers directly reject this kind of attitude. They reject intellectuals, students, and ministers who have that attitude.

But ironically, these same laborers can be seen imitating those whom they have rejected. One who watches the laborers carefully will find them engaged in irresponsible criticism of the other side, drinking, smoking, and cursing. Suddenly they have become intellectualized laborers. It is a distorted image, just like I found when I was in the factory. Sometimes they feel contemptuous of other laborers in their hearts; and they may feel somewhat superior to the other laborers, because they have learned a lot during the movement period and received recognition from the movement people. So their attitude when meeting real factory workers may cause these others to feel ignorant and oppressed. It is a self-contradiction. Have they forgotten they were the same as the other workers, closed and unawakened? If they see fellow workers in such a situation should they not feel empathy, try to come close to them, humble themselves and walk with them? We should gather together all the workers from the bottom, as our comrades, but some movement workers are frustrated and begin action first. In this case the other workers will say immediately, "Well, where did they come from? Aren't they from UIM? Somebody must be behind this." At the same time, the movement workers will be fired, watched, and their names placed on the black list. And after such trouble, a worker might feel self-pride, as if she had gotten a badge of rank in the movement category — even if this incident has no effect on the movement. If I point out this problem to the person involved, she cannot say anything. I can read her mind in detail because I have experienced it myself. One must throw away such an attitude. Self-pride over being a little more educated and conscientized and having experience in the movement should not become a wall between us and those we want to work with.

I came to understand with my body why Jesus came to us as a human being. For us to be saved, that was the only way. Only if he was in such a low position could he achieve his salvation work. I knew this in my heart through my last experience working at the factory. I am reminded of what Dr. Ahn Byung

Mu told me some time ago. It was a few years ago when he was imprisoned at Seodaemoon Prison. One morning he heard the sound of a church bell outside. Usually it was nothing special for him, but that morning the ringing bell moved him tremendously and he was very surprised by this. In his lonely and painful situation the sound of the bell gave him indescribable peace and comfort. He knew many people complained about the noise of church bells and he was one of them: the church bell made nothing but noise; what century are we in, that we still cling to such bell-ringing? He had even suggested removing his own church's bell tower for the community's sake. But now, that very bell sound had given him such comfort and strength! Here he became aware of a very important thing. "Aha! Jesus shows himself to the person who is ready to accept him, in that person's own situation and at his own level."

Once when Jesus healed a blind man, he spat, mixed his spit with dirt, and applied it to the man's eyes. It might look like superstition, but this scene is very important. In today's words, Jesus used the people's way. Why should he use such a method? Jesus could heal the blind without using such a method. It was because that was the people's level.

In conscientization work too, one should not use language at one's own level, but start at the level of the people to be conscientized. The lower the people's socio-economic level, the greater the effect of this method. In the poorer community, the forms of social customs and traditions dominate more strongly than the contents; therefore one can reach and change people better through methods relating to those forms. From this perspective Jesus used a very appropriate method. What we need is this attitude of Jesus. We must learn the people's life and their language, and start from there. Even for me, this is very difficult, as it seems to be for students and laborers also. But we must overcome the difficulty through continual self-training. That is the only way we can renew the movement through the 1980s.

21

Celibacy and Salvation

I THINK IT IS THE SAME in other countries as in Korea, that when a woman has her own active life it is easier to be single. That is because if she marries she will have a husband and children for whom she must make a home, and it is customary for her to be tied to that home. Recently, young women who are involved in the social movement have experienced serious agony over the question of marriage and celibacy, considering our social structure and traditional customs that continue to hinder women's liberation. Probably because of this situation my beloved younger friends ask me, "Reverend, if I want to live like you should I be celibate?" Among laborers with whom I have worked and lived, when one reaches the age of marriage and finds a good man, she wants to get married. When this happens she feels a little guilty and uncomfortable toward me. "Reverend, what shall I do? It looks like I might get married.... You know Mr. Kim, don't you? What do you think of him? If you don't like him, shall I break the engagement?..."

People see me as a confirmed celibate and therefore think that following my life means to be single. Am I a confirmed celibate? Actually I have never given it special thought, and even now I do not insist on being single. But my being alone even after age fifty has made people think of me as celibate. Sometimes I ask myself why I never married. Thinking back, I can find several reasons.

One is that deep in my heart there is a memory that made me disgusted with men. I overcame some of this feeling in the process of my social activities, but it has still not disappeared completely. It was when I was in grade school. My eldest sister, who had been married not long before, came back home crying and carrying a sack of her belongings. She did not want to return to her husband's home.

The problem was that her husband was a dissipated person. He stayed out more than in, and when out he was playing around with other women. My sister had been married hurriedly because of the Japanese policy of taking Korean virgins for "army comforters" (i.e., to provide sexual services to the Japanese soldiers). During that period many Korean virgins were married off hastily to escape such a fate. My sister was thus a victim of the Japanese policy. Although our mother did not have time to choose her son-in-law carefully, she never dreamed he would be so bad — he had looked so gentle and kind. Our faithful Christian home had never seen the likes of such a thing. But a married daughter was an outsider (according to Korean Confucian tradition), so mother had to send my sister back to her new home. When my sister was chased out of our house, I felt like she was being dragged to the slaughterhouse, just like a cow. I pitied her and hated my brother-in-law intensely. I decided that when I grew up I would not marry. My sister came home from time to time and sometimes she had venereal disease passed on by her husband. Mother found penicillin, which was very expensive at that time, and treated her. This shocking childhood memory stayed with me and I hated men for a long time. But as I grew up this feeling lessened.

The second reason has to do with my youthful commitment to God that I would live for my people. Probably it was the influence of my church life that led me to such a decision. I put this decision into action by setting as my goal working in the rural development movement, to which I decided to contribute my life. I thought marrying before I achieved this task would be a betrayal.

Besides these reasons, my puritan lifestyle and thought patterns also had a great influence. And one more reason is that I could not find a man I wanted to marry. As I mentioned before, my love for one man lasted for twenty years without any result, and after that there was nobody who attracted me.

But all these reasons are not real reasons for my celibacy.

Actually, I just happened to be single all this time. Celibacy or marriage — such things were not in my thoughts at all. I just lived sincerely, following the way God gave for my life. If anyone asked me now if I was willing to marry, I would say yes, because I have never intended to be celibate. Actually, when I think about getting old, sometimes I wish for a peaceful refuge. However, I think marriage should not be for the sake of marriage only, but should really be a whole partnership between the two who love one another.

Not long ago some young workers visited me and we played games, including one popular among the young, "ring fortune-telling." A hair from one's head is tied on a gold ring which is swung up and down as many times as one's age, and strangely, the ring spins around and around wildly when it reaches the predicted age of marriage. Mine started spinning on sixty-seven. Marriage at sixty-seven! It seems impossible, but if I do find someone I would like to marry, then I will marry. But no matter how I think about it, I don't believe such a thing will happen.

Ψ

Today the young generation of the movement loves to use the term "revolution." We cannot deny that "revolution" is certainly a word that gives us strength and passion. It is a beautiful thing that young people are ready to commit themselves willingly to the righteous cause of revolution. But one thing causes me concern. That is, the contents of this revolution lean too much to the side of social structural revolution.

Something I felt during the time I was involved in the labor and political movements is that our soul as a movement group is too dry. But we must not let this be, because we are to be the seedbed for the new society we are anticipating and the new order Jesus proclaimed. What this means, religiously speaking, is the formation of the true human being through continuous self-repentance before God, and philosophically speaking, the creation of new being through the inner revolution of the self. In the new age, a new human being is needed. That is because the new world must be realized through change, not only of its form but of its real core.

The new human will be the bridgehead supporting the quality

of the new society. Not only that, but the whole ongoing process
of revolutionary movement must be accompanied by such an
inner revolution. There was a time when I knew nothing about
social movement and thought narrow-minded personal salvation
was the only way. Then, from the time I became involved in
industrial mission, the social salvation aspect was emphasized
and for awhile I thought social movement was all. But now I
have turned around again and realized the necessity to unite
the two sides. Outer social-structural change and change of the
inner human being must proceed together. If one of the two
is lacking, the revolution that the young people desire will be
crippled.

In this sense I have never seen another teacher as great as
Jesus. In Jesus' time there were many lines of movement for
the liberation and independence of Israel. In the case of the
Zealots, they advocated revolution through political struggle.
They felt an urgency to finish everything in a short time. On the
other hand, there were groups like the Essenes who expected to
achieve salvation through their ascetic life in separation from
others. And yet others were like the Pharisees. It is highly un-
likely that Jesus never thought about revolution. But we can
distinguish Jesus from all the other revolutionaries. How? He
proclaimed "Repent, the Reign of God is at hand." Repent. It
is the answer. Be born again as a new person. New wine in
new wineskins. The Reign of God is fundamentally different
from the present world. The new society is a breaking of the
whole present evil circle. This was the unique liberation theory
of Jesus. Some say Jesus was not a revolutionary, basing their
rationale on his use of the word "repent." But this is not true.
Jesus told his disciples to "prepare your swords" before they
faced the enemy.

Jesus' liberation is a movement for the simultaneous achievement of social revolution and the inner revolution of the person.
It is indeed a revolution to create the new future. In this sense
prayer is very important. Jesus prayed before he began anything. He prayed at times of hardship, agony, and temptation.
Purifying one's inner self through prayer makes one able to see
clearly what God's work is. It gives strength against fatigue. In
the case of the non-Christian movement worker, prayer may be
expressed as self-reflection. The continuous effort to objectify

oneself before God and to be faithful before God and history is what creates real love and achieves real revolution. The social revolution, democratization, and human rights movements we are advocating must be actions coming from such inner sincerity. In this sense I want our movement to be a praying movement or a praying revolution.

Recently I read a book, *For Kindred Minds.* It is a diary written by a Bolivian youth, Nestor Paz, about his faith and struggle in the midst of his life in the guerrilla movement. This book impressed me deeply. The people, God, and his own self are united in love, and his struggle really springs from his love.

I think the road we are walking is wide, its destination far. It is a process not only of rejecting the established system, but of creating the new order. We who are involved in the movement should lead the way in becoming persons of the new future.

22

The Women's Movement

IT HAS NOW BEEN TWENTY YEARS since I became involved in
the labor movement through industrial mission and active in
the political movement, and I am already fifty-one. 1984 was
a turning point for me, as I left the Inchon Urban Industrial
Mission after my eighteen-year immersion there and returned
to the pastorate of Dalwol Church, which I had left to begin UIM work. Since it is a rural church it is very quiet and
I can find the space to think about various things. Lately I
am reflecting back on my twenty years of social activities, and
as a result I feel the urgent need of a strong women's movement.

This is probably because I participated in the movement as
a woman. The thing that caused me continual pain for twenty
years was the unequal treatment of women. I also experienced
the agony of discrimination and alienation caused by "sexism."
Women are oppressed wherever we go — at home, at work, in
society, and even before the law. The "have-not" class gets continuously poorer and more oppressed, and yet among those suffering people the most alienated and oppressed of all are the
women. Mothers in the slum areas have more *han* (suppressed
feeling of injustice) than their husbands or sons. Women laborers in the factories are working under worse conditions and
getting less pay than their male counterparts. But the women
laborers' suffering does not stop at the physical level; they also
endure severe mental stress. The cultural climate with its long-
accumulated habits of discrimination against women attempts
to rationalize sexism. Especially in Korea, this discrimination
has deeper roots because of the Confucian thinking that "man
dominates woman" and "woman must follow three ways" (i.e.,
as a child she obeys her father; as a wife, her husband; and as a
mother, her own son).

I think the women's movement has a character that is inclusive, that is social-cultural, and at the same time cannot help being political. Women are the most oppressed class in this society historically, as well as under the capitalist economic structure. Working women are probably the class that has borne the greatest burden of historical oppression created by human society up to now. That is why I think their struggle is most important for the real freedom and liberation of our society. Because of its inclusiveness, the women's movement should of course be developed wherever sexism exists, but the women laborers' movement is especially important and other women's movements should be in solidarity with it.

True human liberation can be accomplished only when the women's liberation movement is realized at the same time. The working class is generally said to be the most important class in solving the contradictions of capitalistic society, and it is thought that human liberation will be achieved through the laborers' struggle. But we must think not only in terms of laborers: we must also think in terms of women and their liberation. Women's oppression does not exist only in theory, and the women's liberation movement is not a by-product of some other movement. However, men usually think like that. Amazingly, even among movement workers many think like that. Women bear a historical task that is twice as hard and important as men's, because women have the additional task of the women's issue on top of all the same work that men must accomplish. Accordingly, women need more autonomy, more ability and skill, and more persistent fighting power. Women have to stand for their own freedom until the end.

Recently I am thinking that our women's movement should proceed more systematically. Without organized power, one cannot win. Further, women must organize themselves carefully because they face many problems in relation to the overall political and labor movements. In the political movement group or labor movement group, a woman's opinion is often ignored or marginalized by the men. No matter how hard she tries to be heard, she will be pushed away from the center against her will and eventually be left out completely. This kind of thing happens quite often. I myself have had such experiences. And the wounds from these experiences are very deep. I am now gathering such wounded women together. Other women movement leaders have had the same kind of experience. There is increasing concern about this situation not only among the members of the women's movement in general but also in the labor movement.

I believe we should have an inclusive, organized women's movement that includes the grassroots women laborers' movement. Such a movement will not only open up a new future to ourselves as women, but will lead the way to the true liberation of all humankind.

$$\Psi$$

There are two levels of dealing with women's issues. One is on the intellectual level and the other on the experiential level. I knew of the issue for some time, but when I had the painful experience of being discriminated against for being a woman, I began to realize the necessity of the women's movement to form women's organizations to empower individual isolated women. Alone a conscientized woman is powerless and suffers endless frustration. It is almost impossible for her to join the large renewal movement if it works as a structured organization, whether it be a church or a secular movement. The only way to break through the established male world is to have organized collective power.

Among the UIMs no other woman was involved when I was, and I was needed by the majority male colleagues like seasoning to food, or so to speak as the necessity of rarity. It was when I was ending my work in the UIM that I felt I was alone. I discovered that the male solidarity that works as group caucuses, protecting and taking care of each other, did not apply to me. I felt the necessity of forming a female power group. And I discovered that as women we did not have such a pressure group of a political nature.

The males established in the status quo looked for me when they needed assistance. When they became self-sufficient and they could do without my help, they no longer wanted me.

Women working with the National Council of Churches in Korea go through the same experience. That's the reason why we formed "The Women with Democracy, People and Nation." Now NCC asks two representatives of women in the democratic movement to participate in their decision-making process on a regular basis.

Individual capability does not count in the organizational structure. Only organized power can give life to an individual as well as to the movement. I was with the UIM for eighteen years and yet it did not occur to my male colleagues to give me a farewell party. It is a concrete example. There is no other way but that we women must work together!

Women are relatively uncorrupt and clean and sincere in their work. As we formed women workers' unions and faced attacks from male union members, I realized the urgent need for a larger scale women's organization that can work as a solidarity network on the problems these suffering women's movements face as they march toward humane treatment. In retrospect I recall numerous experiences of sexism. However, then I was not conscious. When the awareness is raised, the same reality takes on a different face. Now I have crossed the bridge of no return.

23

Dalwol Church Again

AT THE END OF 1984 I finished my work at Inchon Urban Industrial Mission after eighteen years. There were several complex reasons for my resignation, but the most important was that from my standpoint, my role in the labor movement was no longer important, and even if it was, I must not continue in the same way. I was needed in the beginning. I cried with the laborers and rejoiced with them, as we found out the problems together. I was needed when the unconscientized laborers began their first struggle — but that was the level of our laborers at an earlier time. Now they have developed and grown. Now the labor movement needs competent new professional leaders. If one person stays too long and tries to handle everything it limits the development of the movement. But the sad thing is that there is no one with my kind of experience who can continue leadership in the next stage. I am already inadequate for that next stage.

Whoever is involved in the labor movement as an intellectual should have pre-training through sharing the real life of the laborers. There are many cases of persons from the student movement being involved in the labor movement, and their desire is good, but the problem is that they try to lead the labor movement in student movement style. The labor movement field has a different character from that of the student movement. Laborers' place of life is different from that of students or intellectuals. Young people are showing a negative reaction toward our training program since they think it is too old a method. But the content of that training is very valuable, since it is the result of much experience of living and suffering together with the laborers. Of course it is not necessary to keep the movement style exactly as before; in newly developing situations it is necessary to have new methods. But it is important to learn from history because it is what enriches the development of the present.

There were many problems with my moving back to Dalwol Church. I could have moved into another institution after leaving industrial mission, but I chose pastoral work due to my continuing concern for grassroots expansion of the people's movement. I know institutional work is important, but institutions have many limitations. I like to work with "people at the bottom"; it fits me better. But for a person like me, made famous by industrial mission, it is difficult to find a local church. Our still conservative churches in Korea do not call radical ministers like me. It is true that danger exists. That is the reason why few industrial mission pastors have succeeded in local church ministry. I myself barely had my wish come true. I think that God made it possible.

Ψ

I was appointed to Dalwol Church, and I found the church split in two. I somehow expected that, but it was worse than I had thought it would be. They entertained deepest suspicion toward the new pastor.

I saw the necessity to change my image. By hard work and embracing both the opposition and supporting groups without any discrimination, I have brought unity among the congregation.

I had to break the stereotype image that the congregation had of human rights pastors. Their criticism of us is that we do not make home visitation or pray hard. We are only interested in social issues. In order to overcome this criticism I tried my best to meet the congregations' expectations. I stuck with the rural congregation for one year, not participating in any of the movement activities in Seoul. I concentrated on making visitations and praying with the congregation.

The basic principle of all renewal movement is to be sincere and dutiful in one's own situation and given responsibilities. I learned this from the workers. The pastor must not be discriminatory. Disregarding the difference in their economic or social status or educational standard, he or she must love the congregation wholeheartedly. This was the key to overcoming prejudice.

The pastor must address the congregation through the Bible.

Social science might work for intellectuals, but in the early church it was the power of the gospel alone that evangelized people in their total life situations. In most Korean church situations I find the context similar to the early church.

Having had a staunch fundamentalist background, testimony of faith means a lot to me. By experience I found out that church sermons must not be analytical. Through biblical words one can say all she or he wants to say.

When I go on home visitations I use the testimonial approach. I select biblical verses and tell the stories of my own faith experience. I make diligent church offerings and keep up all the standards of the faithful that my congregation has set up. I participate in early morning prayer meetings. Having done all these diligently and conscientiously observed them, I let the people make their own judgment.

During every Passion Sunday we have the foot-washing ceremony. The first year I as the pastor did the foot-washing of twelve elders. As I washed each one's feet I prayed fervently for that person, mentioning all the life situations he or she was in. As I prayed I wept for love, and all the congregation cried as they prayed. I think it was the initial and decisive event of overcoming their prejudice against me.

Each year the foot-washing ceremony takes a different form. For example, we did one slightly different from the first one. The pastor washed the elders, the elders washed the deacons and deaconesses, the deacons and deaconesses washed the lay people. So everybody was involved in the act.

When I administer communion, I do it on the basis of the family unit. I listen to the stories of each family, including the children, and I pray for them. I try my best to have everybody involved in sacraments and worship.

ψ

Once we gathered the unified support of the congregation, the church's programs for the society have been able to progress without much controversy. We now have three major programs. They are the Farmers' Credit Union, a Community Newsletter, and the Nursery and Kindergarten.

Dalwol Church initiated the Farmers' Credit Union in the

village. But now it is indeed a community project. This world-wide movement was originally founded by the Catholics. It is a self-reliant monetary organization where one can borrow necessary money for the cheap interest rate of 2 percent. The trust is a mortgage, and the community makes all the decisions. The success of the cooperative depends on how diligently people save. I learned about credit unions during my service in Inchon. All the labor movement groups are engaged in such projects.

The total population of this village is about five hundred, with 294 family units and 120 houses. (The extended family system requires fewer houses than the number of family units.) The cooperative is an independent organization. It had about 400 million won capital as of July 1986. The chairperson of the Board of Trustees is an elder and the manager is also an elder of Dalwol Church. The church and the community work together very well.

In the village where the church is located people have nothing to read. The newspapers do not come in regularly. In order to give some meaningful reading materials to the people and educate them on national problems, the church publishes a weekly newsletter. We print 400 copies and distribute them to every one of the 294 family units. The rest we send to other rural areas. Mostly menfolk read it. Among women we find many cases of illiteracy.

In the first edition we included words of congratulation from the headman of the county along with the prayer of a farmer. There was some opposition in the beginning, saying, "What will befall us if we make our stance clear from the beginning?" But we made it clear from the very beginning. There might be some unsurfaced opposition, but as of now everybody seems to accept and appreciate it.

In the beginning many believed that the church must deal with only spiritual matters. But when they are conscientized they change their views. I hear village people say: "Please don't leave us here, Reverend."

Presently I am preoccupied with the question, "How do I help the villagers to enter into the struggle of farmers?" We have not yet come to that stage. Historically the people of this area had never had the experience of becoming involved in farmers' rights issues.

Sometimes the county headman comes to see me. He comes escorted by several others. I, by nature, have an abhorrence of those who consider themselves better than others. The pastors before me went to bow down to the county headman, but with me they see a different picture. It is the county headman who comes to see me and I talk to him with no sense of fear. I deliver my frank opinions about present affairs of the society. The villagers who have been intimidated by the government authorities for no reason see a different way of approach to the authorities. They are learning about citizens' rights in a concrete context.

As for the nursery and kindergarten, we have now thirty-five children with two childcare workers. We receive fees of 7,000 won (about $9) per month. We try our best to provide the best learning situation for the children. Our aim is to have childcare workers organize other such workers in the area.

In Inchon 5,600 workers have been organized, and we set up a UIM Supporters' Association. It is important to have conscientized teachers for the young children's education in order to build up a positive self-image about farming and laboring. The aim is that the children respect their farming and factory working parents. With the development boom those who have money and access to success get all the envy and attention of the society, and the working-class people are not only suffering from hard work and economic poverty, but from the contempt of the society. Therefore they have a low self-image. It is hard to be children of the poor and despised. The effort of self-image building is necessary for these children.

Ψ

Because Dalwol Church is rural, it has different problems from the labor area, but the fundamental nature of the problems is the same and they are interconnected. I now have a new desire. Now the parts of pastoral work that most concern me are the church renewal movement, the lay movement, and dialogue with youth. Youth are the most important people, wherever we are. How happy I am to meet and talk with them! Not having had much chance previously to meet grassroots people, having been isolated and under surveillance, now when I talk with the pure and simple people whose lives are filled with suffering, I sometimes wonder, "Am I dreaming, or is this real?"

I am still very cheerful and childish. Contacting new things, I feel excitement and joyful curiosity. My mind is still young. I will probably live another fifteen or twenty years — maybe even another thirty years. If I do not fall ill with a terminal disease or die in an accident, I will live at least fifteen years more. That would be about the same length of time I spent in the social movement. I believe I will be able to do whatever work the Lord gives me. The Lord uses me always as his servant, and I am ever thankful for his grace. I will follow the way he shows me and will live the life he wants me to live, until I die. I thank him for my whole life up to now.

REFLECTIONS

Industrialization and Women: The Social Background of Cho Wha Soon's Ministry

Lee Hyo Jae

THE HISTORICAL CONTEXT OF REV. CHO WHA SOON'S MINISTRY is the process of industrialization occurring in Korea. Her call to the Urban Industrial Mission, for example, came during the initial stages of the industrialization effort launched by the late president Park Chung Hee.

Korean industrialization must be understood in the light of the unique situation of Korea as a divided nation. Through its rapid industrialization over the last two decades, South Korea has become tightly integrated into the world capitalistic system as a peripheral partner, in a relationship dependent on the U.S. militarily, politically, and economically. This dependence began with the U.S. military occupation of South Korea after the Japanese surrender in World War II, according to the agreement made by the allied superpowers that the U.S. and the U.S.S.R. partition the country at the 38th parallel.

The Republic of Korea, thus created, was recognized by the U.N. in 1948 as an independent state. A political and economic system eventually emerged with a pro-American indigenous leadership supported by the conservative sector of the society.

In the meantime, the North established a communist state under the occupation of the U.S.S.R. and in June 1950 initiated military aggression with the self-justified goal of the liberation of the South. Internecine warfare left the divided nation in a state of animosity and continuing conflict. In the South, this allowed further justification of social conservatism and an increased emphasis on national security against the communist North.

The constitution of the new Republic guaranteed equal political, economic, and educational rights to women, but these were strictly nominal. The conservatism of the society did not allow for institutional changes to the Confucian-based patriarchal family system, changes that would have provided a democratic basis for family relations and sexual equality. The new civil laws maintained the basic system of patrilineal succession, discriminating against women in kinship relations and in the inheritance system as well. Although women leaders and organizations voiced strong criticisms, demanding that equality in family relations be guaranteed by the family law, their efforts were of little avail and only minor changes were made. Since 1974, women's organizations have conducted campaigns for the amendment of the discriminatory laws, but their demands are still resisted by the male-dominated conservative legislature.

The Korean family system has served to maintain the cultural tradition of authoritarianism and sex discrimination. Choi Jang Jip, in explaining the functional relation of Korean Confucian culture to the rapid industrialization, states, "Korean culture has nurtured social norms and values that foster a non-conflictual, harmonious society that parallels and reinforces the conception of a strong, bureaucratic state capable of depressing class or interest conflicts as such. This mitigated the destabilizing effects of rapid industrialization [during the Park regime]." An additional legacy of the Confucian tradition is its impact on the formation of a self-educated and hard-working labor force, advantageous to industrialization.

The Park Chung Hee regime, which seized power through the military coup of 1961, effectively used the patriarchal tradition to strengthen its power in an authoritarian-bureaucratic state. Park's educational and cultural policies emphasized the traditional ideology of loyalty and filial piety, granting official awards to self-sacrificing women, faithful daughters-in-law, and virtuous wives. The creation of such a cultural milieu justified the social conditions under which the state mobilized women as a cheap labor force, which sacrificed itself for national industrialization. International observers have noted that few Third World countries can match Korea in terms of the central role of the state in industrial development.

As soon as Park took over power, his regime began to seek the legitimacy of his leadership through economic development for the people, under the slogans of "liberation from poverty" and "self-sufficiency and independence from the U.S. aid economy." It introduced a series of Five-year Economic Development Plans unprecedented in Korea's history. But these ambitious plans had to depend on the strategy of outward-looking development. This strategy focused on labor-intensive light industries in the 1960s and the early 1970s, and then capital intensive heavy industries in the late 1970s until Park's regime collapsed after his assassination in 1979.

In spite of Park's original intention to build a self-sufficient national economy, the export-oriented economy had to depend on foreign capital, technology, and resources. Also, the division of the Korean peninsula was a fatal blow to the development of an integrated economy, cutting off the natural basis for regional cooperation between the agricultural South and the industrial North, between the South's light industry and the North's heavy industry. And thus the state had to induce massive foreign capital in direct and indirect investment for the promotion of industrialization.

This economic drive resulted in an impressive record of industrialization in the 1960s and 1970s. High uninterrupted economic growth was achieved, accounting for an annual average growth rate of 9.2 percent in the GNP. The contribution of manufacturing industries to economic growth was increased from 13 percent to 60 percent in the same period. The labor-intensive export industries based on the abundant low-wage labor force, particularly young single women, showed impressive growth: from 1962 to 1979 Korea's exports soared from $55 million to $15 billion, raising the yearly mean export growth rate to 45 percent.

The focus of industrialization has changed from traditional light industries to modern heavy industries. In this process, the proportion of the labor force in manufacturing nearly tripled. However, this rapid growth of export industrialization inevitably led the Korean economy into deepening dependency on foreign trade and investment. The import of raw materials and capital goods has increased dramatically.

In foreign trade, the U.S. and Japan are South Korea's two major trading partners. South Korea's deficit in the balance of trade has widened, necessitating increased foreign capital. South Korea has thus become heavily indebted; with debt of over $40 billion in 1984, it was the fourth largest debtor country in the world.

Dependent development has produced impressive growth, bringing new recognition of South Korea's status and role: from a peripheral agrarian state to the semi-periphery of the international capitalistic system. Internally, however, it has caused decisive changes in the social structure, with widening gaps in income distribution and consumption levels.

The low-wage policy for labor in export industries has excluded the working class from their share of economic growth, evident in unequal income distribution and the decrease in real wages: In 1984, 88 percent of the workers employed in manufacturing received wages below the minimum cost of living. As for single workers, of which 59 percent were single women, 71 percent received a wage below the minimum cost of living. In a 1983 comparison with Taiwan and Singapore, South Korean workers showed the lowest average monthly wage: South Korea, 100; Taiwan, 126; Singapore, 156. South Korean workers worked more hours per week (54.3 hours) than workers in those other two Asian countries.

Such exploitative working conditions, with the worst discrimination against women workers, make it clear why women workers had to engage in fierce labor struggles during the 1970s under the oppression of the Park regime.

Thus the industrialization plan of South Korea was founded on the cheap labor of its people. The workers, most of them from rural areas, suffer from low wages, bad working conditions, and no unionization. Women workers suffer more because of the added burden of the patriarchal culture, which rationalizes exploitation of all the powerless, especially women. Most women workers are young, single women from rural areas who help with their family's living expenses and the education of their brothers.

With urbanization and industrialization, the whole nation has been going through rapid social change, and the poorest and the powerless have had to bear the brunt. In this social whirlpool Rev. Cho Wha Soon was called to work for the women factory workers by the Urban Industrial Mission. Her decision to go was not simple, especially since she was enjoying an established ministerial post at a local congregation, not common for women pastors in Korea.

Her preference to be where nobody else wanted to go has begun a new chapter for the mission of the Korean church, for the labor movement, and especially for women's role in the unions. In the Dong-il Textile Company, where Rev. Cho ministered, women workers organized themselves and elected a woman union leader for the first time in the history of their labor union. She was the second woman in Korea to become a union leader.

Rev. Cho now works in a rural church ministering to farm families. As the farmers encounter problems stemming from the rapid industrialization of the export-oriented economy, Rev. Cho brings them good news.

Lee Hyo Jae *is professor of sociology at Ewha Women's University in Seoul; she is actively involved with the issues of democratization, reunification, and human rights for working women.*

Korean Women's Reflection

Ahn Sang Nim — Kim Hai Won
Kim Soon Myoung — Lee Sun Ai
Nam Myoung Hee

A group of women, all members of the Korean Association of Women Theologians, were organized by Ahn Sang Nim to read the story of Cho Wha Soon and reflect on it together. Included here is an edited version of their conversation,

Ahn Sang Nim: I think the ministry of Rev. Cho Wha Soon has historical significance for the life of church and society in Korea. The Protestant churches in Korea commemorated the centennial of their mission in 1985. The Korean church has undergone many ordeals politically and economically, with socio-cultural and theological consequences. Now it has become a self-supporting and missionary-sending church. However, as we are marching into the second century of mission, we would like to raise the question regarding the nature of the mission of the church. Have we done or are we doing enough for justice issues in church and society? For example, are we adequately dealing with human rights issues, including those for women? In this regard Rev. Cho is one of those who have opened up new ways of mission, not only in words but in deed and life.

Her most striking aspect for me is her motherly love toward women workers, which made her stand firmly with them against the cruel exploitation of the capitalist managers and struggle with them for their rights and human dignity. It was not an easy task.

Lee Sun Ai: I think you have pointed out something very important. In the 1960s and 1970s most struggling people put priority on political democratization. The human rights struggle in the 1980s can be viewed as more holistic in that it includes economic as well as political democracy, with emphasis on authentic national culture and spirit. In the 1970s Kim Chi Ha and other farsighted people spoke with prophetic voices. They foresaw the inevitable continuation of economic and political exploitation by external forces and internal elites. Increasing militarism is also the consequence of the kind of development planned by Western capitalists and sold to the iron-fisted dictator, the late president Park Chung Hee. The export-oriented industrial models were not people oriented. Still many people were enchanted by the economic miracle that the war-torn nation was achieving.

In this milieu Rev. Cho Wha Soon stood up to fight against the exploitation of powerless women workers. She went to the factory as a worker to identify with them. Nowadays hundreds of young students volunteer to work in the factories, abandoning their hard-won academic life in order to identify with and organize the workers toward a politically and economically self-reliant and unified Korea. Rev. Cho pioneered a ministry for total integration.

I think it was significant that her initial experience of factory work was the occasion for the revelation to her of the full meaning of the doctrine of the incarnation. Her intellectual theological orientation became complete as it converged with the workers' humiliating life situation. The dawning realization of the doctrine of incarnation came as a simple and profound reality only when she lived the incarnated life: the word received in the flesh and for others. The modern compartmentalized way of life and thinking prohibits us from experiencing this fundamental Christian doctrine.

As capitalistic modernization and technological development touch the roots of our way of life, creating a fragmented value system woven into patriarchal-hierarchical control mechanisms, our way of thinking and theologizing are also affected. Our views tend toward a partial, individualistic, male-centered, divisive, authoritarian, and dualistic perspective instead of a holistic, communal, altruistic reaching out toward all-inclusive unity. We will be able to overcome exploitation by means of sexism, racism, and classism and the North-South and the East-West conflicts only if we strive toward such an all-inclusive unity; when we reach our goal justice and peace will flow like a river. Rev. Cho's concrete selfless love of her neighbors who come to her — as the wounded soldiers during the Korean war, women workers in the factory, her own congregation in the church, and any others who come along the path of her life — is the manifestation of her vision. And her vision grew to the point where she had to risk her own security and reputation for the sake of justice. This vision and this way of pioneering ministry reach out and touch hundreds and thousands of hearts creating an epochal tide toward a new heaven and a new earth.

Ahn Sang Nim: As a mother and one who endeavors to pursue feminist theology, I want to see Cho Wha Soon's God as God the mother. This God pours motherly love into the heart of Cho Wha Soon and all those who are transformed by her way to act as great mothers who genuinely care for others as a mother would for her own child.

In 1951 as a young girl of sixteen, she became a war refugee and went to Pusan, the southernmost city of Korea. With other girls who went there with her, she served as a nurse's aid to the wounded soldiers. While the nurse Cho was taking care of the wounded soldiers in the cold of winter, she noticed that none of them had warm socks. Her compassionate heart drove her to find a solution to this need of these helpless people. She found worn out and dirty army blankets in the store room. Not finding any washing facilities in the temporary hospital she went to the creek with the blankets after her duties at night. She broke the ice of the stream and washed them with her freezing hands. When they dried she started to sew socks for each inmate all by herself during the night. How can we explain this unusual act of a sixteen-year-old girl but as a God-inspired act of motherly concern?

In her story she recollects her anguished search for the meaning of life as a teenager. Then she was dreaming of becoming a musician or a dancer. But when she realized the suffering of the Korean people under Japanese colonialism, she changed her mind and led a life of sacrifice and service for others. She responded constantly to the motherly call of God.

Kim Soon Myoung: This story makes me want to quote Mark 14:8–9. "She has done what she could; she has anointed my body beforehand for burying. And truly I say to you, wherever the Gospel is preached in the whole world, what she has done will be told in memory of her."

While the male disciples did not comprehend the coming mystery of the crucifixion and resurrection of Jesus, it was a nameless woman who anointed Jesus in preparation for his death. She dared to go into the male world to do what she believed must be done in spite of not having been invited. All the male disciples did not perceive the significance of what she was doing; Jesus alone saw the true meaning. Like this nameless woman Rev. Cho is a courageous prophet who proclaims the reign of God with all her heart and soul. In other words, with the totality of her being she exercises the power of the love of God as it is written in the Scripture: "You shall love the Lord your God with all your heart, and with all your soul, and with all your mind, and with all your strength" (Mark 12:30).

As a Christian minister, Rev. Cho has executed the mission of God. Cho went to the land of darkness, of the pains and suffering of the unjustly exploited women workers. Living and working with them every day, she protested the contradictions of the social structure. For doing this she was imprisoned and was tortured. Her protest against the low wage policies, the inevitable strategy to promote export industry, is in line with the spirit of the prophetic traditions of the Old Testament and the ministry of Jesus Christ. As the Lord could not help but express angry judgment against those rich who sold the poor for a pair of shoes and who trampled the head of the poor into the dust of the earth (Amos 2:6-7), Rev. Cho also could not help expressing her anger against those businesses that make great profit by exploiting the poor industrial workers. They were paid just a snack-cost wage for a long day's work. Rev. Cho's social criticism was in accordance with the spirit of the prophet Nathan. His criticism against King David, who had despised God's commandments, was expressed in the parable of the ewe lamb of the poor. While the rich man had many flocks and herds and the poor man had only one ewe lamb, the rich man took the poor man's ewe lamb to treat his visitor (2 Sam. 12:1-15).

Nam Myoung Hee: I will speak here from the viewpoint of traditional religious teaching of Korea. To me Rev. Cho comes very close to the concept of Soo Bu (a head woman) of Jeung San Gyo, which was highly developed in Korea in the past century.*

---

*Jeung San Gyo: of the traditional oriental religions, such as Donghak, Won-

Jeung San Gyo views the cosmos as divided into two different eras: Seon Chun and Hoo Chun. In the Seon Chun era the heaven and earth are dominated by the male sex, but Hoo Chun is the era of the future great women who are to be called Soo Bu. They shall appear to correct their ridiculed status and to establish the right female and male relationship, right Yin and right Yang. In this era men shall not execute rights once only theirs without women's permission or consent (Daisun Holy Book 5:134). Jeung San Gyo began in social circumstances of Confucianist-oriented patriarchy. At the end of the Yi Dynasty the fate of the nation was in a critical situation due to the threats and invasions of foreign powers and internal corruption. Jeung San Gyo was promoted as a return to the traditional religions and away from foreign-oriented religions like Buddhism, Confucianism, and Christianity.

In Jeung San Gyo, woman-above-man ideology was traced back to the time of Tangun, the founding ancestor of the Korean nation. In those days, as in other matriarchal cultures, women were the mediators to God.

Kim Hai Won: I would like to speak from the perspective of my prison ministry. In nature God gives sunshine and rainfall equally to the good people and the bad. Perhaps this can be called the universality of God's act. Nevertheless, in the Old and New Testaments, the righteousness of God is always on the side of the weak, the exploited and oppressed, demonstrating concrete acts of judgment, proclaiming recovery of their rights. God regards the orphans, the widows, the sick, the maimed, the homeless wanderers and unfairly treated as righteous people. On the other hand, God warns the oppressors of fatal judgment. True to the tradition of Scripture, Jesus also showed sympathy toward the sinners, the suffering, the poor, the despised and alienated. He performed miracles to heal, feed, and give back life to them and treated them as friends.

Paul became the captive of Jesus Christ and abandoned all

Buddhism, and Daijonggyo, Jeung San Gyo has been most highly developed in Korea. Its dogmas are quite similar to those of Donghak, which means in Korean "Eastern studies" — over against Western Christianity. It advocated the freedom of women from existing social structures, which were based on Confucianism and patriarchalism, and from all dehumanizing conditions.

the privileges he had possessed previously to announce the good news to the Gentile slaves and sinners. Rev. Cho deserves being called a real imitator of Jesus Christ and true follower in deed and in a life that manifests itself in justice and the love of God. She gives all of herself in love for all women workers. They are the real force of industrial production but are not rewarded justly; instead they are caught up in a life of misery and sexual discrimination.

Her mission to these women, far from glamor or social respect, was her own choice. She could have chosen to be a chaplain in a school or missionary to Japan or continue in her pastoral work. But she chose what other people do not want to do, the hard life of the low-class factory workers, living and working with them in order to serve, but not to be served. It is indeed a Christ-like mission.

But through the experience of being insulted and contemptuously treated by the foreman in the work place, she learned the real meaning of the love of Christ, the crucified one. In emptying herself at the feet of this crucified one, she could overcome the insults and impudent treatment of the foreman. She finds God's presence in the situation of the hard work, suffering, and pain of these women as God was present in the silent suffering with the crucified Christ. With the resurrection hope she stays with them, encouraging them, teaching and struggling together with them for a better day.

Because of this mission of incarnation she was imprisoned twice and has been kept under surveillance by the authorities ever since. Once she was sent to prison for violating the Presidential Emergency Decree No. 4. She met a woman imprisoned allegedly for spying for North Korea. This woman was a beautiful human being with a kind and humble heart. This story and other prison experiences she speaks about make us think that dictatorial national laws put angelic persons behind iron bars, while demonic forces are carrying out their destructive dehumanizing policies in broad daylight. In this situation, what does national security really mean?

Our mission to the prisoners must start from full understanding of the prisoner as a human being and as a person who has specific needs like everybody else. Labeling them as criminals and putting them behind bars will not help them be rehabilitated. We can learn much from Rev. Cho's mission and the treatment of the exploited women workers.

Ahn Sang Nim: I want to continue on the theme of God the mother. Leonard Swidler brought up the image of God as a mother in interpreting Genesis 3:21, which says: "The Lord God made for Adam and for his wife garments of skins, and clothed them." In the same vein God's act of creation is seen in the image of maternity. God made coats and clothed Adam and Eve in love. They disobeyed God; still God loved them and demonstrated this in the concrete act of clothing them. Nurse Cho's love for the wounded soldiers was not superficial sentimentalism; it was deeply rooted in the nature of the maternal love of God. Jesus' attitude toward women as it is described in the synoptic Gospels was really open and truly understanding in the midst of the misogynist culture of his time. His attitude toward all the other oppressed peoples also manifested the maternal love of God.

In everyday life in Korea we observe that mothers understand deeper and better the problems of their children than anybody else. I believe it is because of their love. As we read the Bible in this manner, it will encourage many women who seek their own security in a small and closed world of patriarchal negation of their worth as full persons to open their eyes to see the truth and to be involved in God's mission.

The genuine sympathy and love of nurse Cho toward the wounded patients make us affirm the motherly nature of God's love, which lasts forever. She was called by the patients "the respected nurse." Very often the psychological needs of the wounded are forgotten in a war situation. Their dreadful experiences in the front line, the sudden death and bloodshed of their friends, sounds of gunshots and deepest fear of death, are totally ignored, and the loving hands of their mothers cannot reach them. Nurse Cho showed her motherly love that comes from the creator by covering their naked feet. This love must be the instrument of feminist theology. Love of such intensity and sincerity, which unites all for the cause of renewal of human community, is urgently needed as we envision and work toward a new heaven and a new earth.

Kim Soon Myoung: We have mentioned Rev. Cho's experience of humiliation and her love. Perhaps we should also bring

up the situations of dehumanization that these women workers are going through. Whenever they demand their rights in a
peaceful manner such as a work slow-down, a peaceful strike,
negotiations between the parties involved, they are rewarded by
police with rape, imprisonment, torture, and being put on the
black list so that they will never be hired again by other companies, which is the denial of their livelihood. They have even
had human excrement poured all over their bodies and forced
into their mouths. This last incident occurred when they tried
to organize a union meeting. They were not involved in any act
of protest.

Moreover, women workers suffer long working hours, poor
conditions, low wages, and humiliating treatment by supervi-
sors. Rev. Cho's mission in this circumstance is like what is said
in Micah 6:8: "God has shown you, O man [and woman], what
is good; and what does the Lord require of you, but to do justice,
and to love kindness, and to walk humbly with your God." The
prophetic spirit revealed by Rev. Cho's industrial mission could
be summed up in three points. First, she denounced the injustice done to women workers by living with them. Second, she
exposed the injustice and violence that had been justified and
covered up by the corrupt powers. Third, she strongly asserted
the recovery of human rights and better treatment of women
workers in the belief that every human being is created in the
image of God.

Nam Myoung Hee: As I said before, I like to see Rev. Cho
as a Soo Bu, the head woman. In 1966 she started the Urban Industrial Mission work at Dong-Il Textile Company. There
she found out that the traditional method of evangelism was no
longer relevant to the salvation of the women workers in such
a situation of discrimination and exploitation. In a very low-
key way she started consciousness-raising education, which led
the women to elect one of their own as the chief of their labor
union. The Soo Bu Cho Wha Soon was making more Soo Bus
where she was. This was the first woman union leader in Korea's labor history. In 1974, imprisoned on the charge of the
violation of the law against meetings and demonstrations, she
cried out aloud to break down evil social structures. She said,
"We will fight against the evils of this land. The resentment
and grudges of all the oppressed and alienated poor women will

become the power to bring the judgment of God upon those oppressors!"

The nature and way of Rev. Cho's mission indeed corresponds to the Jeung San Gyo's era of Hoo Chun, the idealistic era in which the "right female, right male" relationship is established and the *"han"** of oppressed women is resolved as they walk in the era of equality between men and women. Rev. Cho's struggle for this era in this conservative patriarchal culture aims for cosmic transformation and the construction of a new culture.

Lee Sun Ai: I want to elaborate on Kim Hai Won's perspective of prison ministry. In fact, currently Korea is undergoing imprisonment by the superpowers and internal dictatorship, consequences of the division of the nation. There is a widening gap between the few plutocrats and the masses of the poor who strive hard to survive. Deprivation of various kinds of human rights, such as freedom of speech, organization, and fair participation in political decisions, to name a few, is the way of life. Great discrimination and oppression of the female sex, economically, politically, culturally, and religiously, must be overcome if the country really means to join the march of the world community.

Young students and other concerned people continuously stand up boldly for freedom to achieve a truly democratic national life. Rev. Cho has been and still is a very important and significant source in the struggle of all people for freedom, particularly in supporting the industrial workers, who are one-third of the total population of the nation, and women, who are one-half of the population. Rev. Cho identifies with this exploited and deprived people and is committed to raising awareness of what beautiful, kind, and important people they are in their vulnerable and humble situations.

The late Professor Suh Nam Dong's entry point for minjung theology is the *han* of Korean people. Rev. Cho, like the shamans in traditional Korean religion, acts to resolve the op-

---

*Han: resentment or unresolved accumulated frustration. Jeung San Gyo defines the resentments of the oppressed in human culture as fourteen different *hans,* such as the *han* of women, of Hangu I darkened by Chinese, of the traditional folk deity being persecuted in modern culture, etc. It teaches that the utopia will come when the world is released from these *hans.*

pressed and exploited people's accumulated frustration and resentment. She is indeed a minjung theologian. The entry point of Professor Ahn Byung Mu's minjung theology is the multitude (*ochlos*) in the Gospel of Mark. The multitude actively sought Jesus for the good news of the coming Reign of God. The political, economic, and religious oppressions they faced were unbearable. Fully understanding their reality and their aspirations and moved by the most profound compassion of God, which Ahn Sang Nim calls motherly nature, Jesus interacted with this reality, giving solutions to current problems, but always aiming at the utopian Reign of God. His ministry was a costly defiance against all the established systems and their authorities. For his commitment to the Reign of God and loving mission of salvation for all those who suffer, he was crucified. But through the act of God the Almighty he was resurrected. Like the Palestinian *ochlos,* the Korean minjung, the oppressed masses of people, also seek justice and peace in the country with the same urgency of anticipation. The Korean minjung's final vision is no more or no less than the Jewish "reign of the righteous God, the state of Shalom," for this land that suffers legions of wounds of division, and for this people who clamor ceaselessly for justice. To this land and to these people Rev. Cho's mission of total commitment in loving action is dedicated.

The way toward fullness of life and freedom for this country is to fulfill the aspirations of minjung women, men, and their children. Christian mission in this situation is to bring good news of liberation for all the prisoners, both in literal and figurative senses, for all aspects of their lives. Rev. Cho herself has gone through the life of a political prisoner twice and is still living the life of a figurative prisoner with the rest of her compatriots. But she will never be passive. She will continue, with many other conscientious people, to seek for a workable solution for the nation and the people.

Ahn Sang Nim *is general secretary of the Korean Association of Women Theologians and chairperson of the Women's Committee of the Korean National Council of Churches.*

Kim Soon Myoung *is an evangelist of the Methodist church in Seoul.*

Nam Myoung Hee *is a core member of the Feminist Theology Study Group of the Korean Association of Women Theologians.*

Kim Hai Won *works in prison ministry in Seoul.*

Lee Sun Ai *is editor of* God's Image *and is the coordinator of Asian Women's Theology for the Ecumenical Association of Third World Theologians.*

All the contributors are members of the Korean Association of Women Theologians.

The Challenge of
Cho Wha Soon:
A U.S. Perspective

Patricia J. Patterson

Cho wha soon is a remarkable human being. A spell-binding storyteller, she recounts her experiences and those of sister and brother workers with humor, indignation, and prophetic insight. She moves from sighs to laughter, from delight to explosions of anger with a wholeness that is intensely attractive and involving. The integrity of her living and speaking is a constant.

I met her first in July 1972 in the big thatched roof farmhouse in Inchon where Urban Industrial Mission (UIM) was headquartered. She was full of the excitement of the first victory of women workers to elect women labor union leaders. After meeting the new president of the Dong Il Textile Union, we prayed and ate together, the simple meal of soup and rice and many kinds of *kimchi*. That was the beginning of what has been nearly two decades of meeting Rev. Cho and courageous union leaders from time to time and of being deeply moved by their stories of struggle, achievement, suffering, anger, and strength.

But as an American Christian woman, I have found the encounters and the stories often disturbing. As the Korean context for the labor struggle, especially among women workers, has become clearer to me, the role of the United States and U.S. companies in being supportive of structures of exploitation and oppression in Korea has also become clear. The friendship of many South Koreans, fortified by U.S. assistance in the Korean War and aid in rebuilding the Republic of Korea, has been eroded in recent years by U.S. government support for two military dictatorships and by U.S. policy decisions to choose national security over human rights and democracy in Korea. What appears to be emerging for many concerned Koreans is a picture of U.S. self-interest at the sacrifice of Korean self-reliance and democratic reform.

One embassy official in Seoul in the early 1980s said: "South Korea has built its economy in large measure on the backs of teenage women workers." The rapid industrialization of South Korea in the late sixties, seventies, and eighties has followed the export model of development. It has required great capital investment from abroad and cheap labor, stability, and security from within. With agriculture increasingly neglected in government policy and with imports of food, including rice, as well as of costly fertilizers and pesticide, from the U.S. and other countries encouraged, the farm economy has suffered. Young people, especially women, have been pushed out of the unprofitable countryside and pulled into the rapidly expanding cities with their industrial centers, sweatshops, and slums. To help feed their families and pay the school fees for younger brothers and sisters, teenage girls have flocked to the cities for jobs in the factories. Living in company dormitories or tiny rooms where they sleep in shifts, working 10–12 hours a day and 28–30 days a month in unhealthy and often unsafe working conditions, with low pay, harassment by male bosses, and intense weariness, these young women have for more than two decades carried the South Korean economy forward on their backs.

Meanwhile, foreign companies, including American corporations, have made large profits. Democratically elected labor unions in the factories, which were courageously organized in the seventies, were brutally repressed and almost completely destroyed in the early eighties. The union in the Control Data factory was one of the last to be destroyed. Governments of succeeding military dictators have strengthened their control of labor, the media, the political opposition, the education system, and society in general. The emphasis on national security and the threat of North Korean invasion have increased the militarization of the society and provided the rationale for putting down dissent. U.S. military aid and the presence of 40,000 U.S. troops have been seen as strengthening Korean military influence.

What benefits some groups in the United States strangles and destroys some people in Korea. Selling rice and other agricultural products to Korea is good for U.S. farmers, especially agri-business, but it destroys Korean agriculture and the lives of farm families. South Korea, which was almost totally food self-sufficient in 1960, provides only about 50–60 percent of its food in the 1980s. Low wages, the prohibition of independent labor unions, minimal standards of safety in the working environment, and a controlled country benefit multinational corporations. U.S. companies run away from higher wages, better working standards, and organized unions in the U.S. to countries like Korea where their profits are higher and responsibility lower. Meanwhile, Korean workers pay the price for foreign profit and domestic development.

The U.S. military has an elaborate command system and training program in South Korea that furthers the South Korean government's national security objectives. Emphasizing the threat of North Korea and delaying steps that would contribute to reduction of tensions and real peace, both the U.S. and R.O.K. militaries continue to rationalize their expanded role in Korea. Meanwhile, the Korean people remain divided with controlled, military dominated, and undemocratic political systems. The impact of military bases on the lives of women and children and the drain of military budgets on the economy result in increased social problems. Such government policies made by mainly well-to-do men in Korea and the U.S. do not benefit ordinary people.

Analysis of Korea-U.S. relations, economic development, military alliance, industrialization, agricultural deterioration, and political control, however, can be remote and unreal. But sitting face to face with ten fifteen- to eighteen-year-old women who tell their own stories in the midst of these forces makes the price they have paid all too real. "I wish I could go back to my village and finish school. I want to study," says a fifteen-year-old who had to leave school after the eighth grade. "I'm so tired," says another who is having her first day off in three weeks. "I wish I could rest and play with my friends." Others complain of eyestrain, headaches, upset stomachs, and nausea after long hours of peering into microscopes at an electronics factory. But they cannot stop working because their livelihood and that of their rural families depend on them. Cho Wha Soon has taken into herself the pain, the strength, the loving community, and courage of these young people. She has also been for them big sister, labor counselor, and pastor.

Union leaders in the late seventies and early eighties were strikingly strong and able. Graduates of junior high school or sometimes senior high, they were articulate, clear thinking, and sensitively supportive of each other. Some of them were Christians — some Catholics, some Protestants. Their testimonies to faith in Jesus Christ were deeply moving. Their commitment to the struggle for just labor conditions and relations grew out of their faith as well as out of better experience and concern for their fellow workers.

Such witness of faith challenges our lukewarm Christianity. I am uncomfortable in the face of such simply faithful discipleship. Even our prayers are not informed and constant enough, let alone our advocacy and action to change unjust relations. When GE brings good things to us, I remember an assembly line in Korea where young women with aching fingers and fatigued backs and eyes put together lines of Christmas lights for our comfortable homes in the U.S.

But I also know that out of the struggle of labor unions in Korea came the impetus for groups like the North American Coalition for Human Rights in Korea to work in Washington for legislation that would address violations of the rights of workers. In 1984, an amendment on the Generalized System of Preferences was passed. It gives specific trade preferences only to countries that are "taking steps to afford workers the internationally recognized workers' rights." This means that countries that repress their workers do not qualify for tariff-free access to the American market. Such a law is one response to the challenge for just relations that Rev. Cho and tens of thousands of women workers have called for.

Another response is participation by American Christians in the international and ecumenical process initiated by the World Council of Churches to work toward peace and reunification on the Korean peninsula. A divided Korea continues to involve the separation of up to ten million people from their families, to give rationale to political control north and south, and to perpetuate the dangerously tense relations between massive military forces along the Demilitarized Zone. Recognizing that the U.S. has played a major role in the division and continuing separation of

Korea, our work as Christians is to help remove the hindrances that U.S. policy puts in the way of Koreans themselves dealing seriously with issues of democratization, peacemaking, and reunification.

The question that Rev. Cho's ministry continues to raise in me is whether all the world's people can live interdependently without living as exploited and exploiter; whether everyone can have enough, rather than too little for many and too much for the few; whether security can be redefined to mean democracy, dignity, equality, mutual respect, and peace, rather than preparation for war, wasted resources for weapons, and paranoia at dissent, which leads to torture, imprisonment, or death.

The struggle in Korea continues. The demonstrations for democratic elections in June 1987 expressed almost as one voice the hunger of the south Korean people for justice and participation. In July and August the workers rose up demanding wage increases and the right to organize unions. The media at first were sympathetic to this first massive labor uprising and demand for political change, but then shifted to attack the workers. They were accused of being communists and gangsters, of mistreating company heads and trying them in people's courts. Company presidents were incensed and demanded an apology, as they claimed that these lies destroyed their honor. The National Managers Association, which levied the charges apologized, to the company heads but not to the workers whose reputation was even more severely damaged.

In September churchpeople, including Rev. Cho Wha Soon, had a four-day prayer meeting and hunger strike at the Human Rights Office of the National Council of Churches of Korea. Afterward they went to the office of the National Managers Association to meet its president and discuss an apology to the workers. They waited for five hours. The police were called, and the church delegation was accused of using violence. Most members of the delegation were soon released, but Rev. Cho and several others were detained. Reflecting on that experience, she says that their action was so mild that she could not imagine that such harsh punishment would be imposed. Apparently as the national presidential election heated up throughout the fall, the government was afraid of Rev. Cho's influence. For nearly three months she was held in solitary confinement. She was released on December 16, the eve of the presidential election.

Cho Wha Soon speaks of imprisoned students with great respect and appreciation. Through their protests, conditions in the prison had improved considerably. Prisoners were given a sponge mattress and blankets, and food was better. She understands their action as a way of struggling toward the Reign of God and as a way of taking seriously Christ's invitation to "ask and you shall receive; seek and you shall find."

Cho Wha Soon's ministry is multi-faceted and whole. In whichever direction she turns in Korean society and the church she brings the Christian faith to bear, the faith that in Acts 17:6 is described as turning the world upside down. She is a local church pastor who involves her entire congregation in ministry and helps create among them leavening community. The church bulletin serves not only as a guide to the church service and congregational activities but as a newsletter for the entire rural community in which the church is located.

Rev. Cho is currently president of the Korea Association of Women Theologians (KAWT) with its nearly 300 theologically trained women of various denominations. KAWT's program includes continuing education for women in ministry and activities furthering women's participation and leadership in the church. She is also vice chair of the Methodist Women Ministers Association, which brings together ordained women and women evangelists. One major focus is on women evangelists who are at the heart of the church's outreach in Korea but who are poorly paid, have little training, and are given little status in the male dominated church structure. Rev. Cho takes the church very seriously both as a faith community witnessing to salvation and new life in Jesus Christ and as an agent for change in society. She participates fully in the annual conference and district activities of the Korean Methodist Church and in various committees of the National Council of Churches in Korea. She is frequently called upon as a very powerful preacher and speaker as well as an able chairperson.

She continues to be actively involved in support of labor and rural movements, carefully respecting and nurturing leadership among farmers and factory workers themselves. Cho Wha Soon is an empowering person. She aims always at enabling people to define their own oppression and liberation and inspiring them to use their talents with collective power. Because women in every facet of Korean life are still at the bottom, she has a special sense of calling to ministries with and among women. Having experienced the unconscious putdown by male colleagues, exclusion from the old boys' network, and marginalization for being involved in social justice ministries, especially involving women, she has a deep sensitivity to women's feelings and status in church and society. She is in tune with the growing realization of many in the Korean democratization movement in Korea that the liberation of Korean women is an integral part of the democratization of the nation.

At the end of Cho Wha Soon's only visit to the United States in the spring of 1986, some of us asked about her impressions of our country. She said, "I did not know that so many people are struggling for justice here in the U.S. too, especially racial and ethnic minorities and women. Your country has often been portrayed to us as a perfect, ideal, golden land of plenty. I am both sobered and enheartened by the fact that we have so much struggle in common. People everywhere need to work together."

Cho Wha Soon remains a powerful witness to the need of people everywhere to work together. In her rural parish, in church structures, with workers and women's movements, she continues to inspire new leadership, challenge people to live out their convictions, and work toward an equal and just society. Connected as we are by both the bonds of oppression and the hopeful struggle for justice and peace, we in the U.S. need indeed to work together for the sake of the Korean people whose liberation is tied to our own.

Patricia J. Patterson *is Northeast Asia Secretary of the United Methodist Board of Global Ministries.*